Sensory Solutions
TRAINING SERIES WITH "DR. TONY"

MSE 03

Creating Meaningful Moments

a training series for working with Individuals and groups in multi-sensory environments

Anthony M. McCrovitz, Ph.D.

MSE 03
Creating Meaningful Moments
All Rights Reserved.
Copyright © 2024 Anthony M. McCrovitz, Ph.D.
First printing, 2024

The opinions expressed in this manuscript are solely the opinions of the author and do not represent the opinions or thoughts of the publisher. The author has represented and warranted full ownership and/or legal right to publish all the materials in this book.

This book may not be reproduced, transmitted, or stored in whole or in part by any means, including graphic, electronic, or mechanical without the express written consent of the publisher, except in the case of brief quotations embodied in critical articles and reviews.

NO AI TRAINING: Without in any way limiting the exclusive rights under copyright of the author and publisher, any use of this publication to "train" generative artificial intelligence (AI) technologies to generate text is expressly prohibited. The author reserves all rights to license uses of this work for generative AI training and development of machine learning language models.

a-pearABLE press
https://editorink.com/a-pearable-press/

ISBN 979-8-218-96299-9
Library of Congress Control Number: 2023919118

Content and Developmental Editor, ©2024 Mara Hawks, MA
http://editorink.com.
All rights reserved - used with permission.

Book series introduction, cover, and interior design by Mara Hawks.
Unless otherwise credited, interior images and artwork produced by Mara Hawks for Quality of Life Institute, Inc. (qualityoflifeinstitute.org.)

PRINTED IN THE UNITED STATES OF AMERICA

OTHER TITLES IN THIS SERIES

SS TRAINING MSE 01
MSE HISTORY AS TOLD BY FOUNDER AD VERHEUL, AND THE 8 MSE FAVORABLE FACTORS

SS TRAINING MSE 02
SENSORY SOLUTIONS FRAMEWORK AND DEVELOPMENT OF THE SENSES

This book is dedicated to

Pouwel van de Siepkamp (1949 – 2023)

dear friend, colleague, and gentle teacher

SENSORY SOLUTIONS, a series of MSE workbooks, arrives at a time when AI (Artificial Intelligence) is entering the forefront of human interactions, giving rise to an increased need for unwavering adherence to core, human values that are the foundation of human identity and cultural integrity.

Integrity dwells in the possibility of loss. The value and meaning of human life becomes known as it is cultivated and celebrated through human interactions. With MSE Sensory Solutions, relationship-building dynamics accelerate the discovery and exploration of meaningful connections with a compass of core human values. Values such as mutual respect, compassion, inclusion, unconditional acceptance, and servant leadership align the work of navigating the heart through conflicts and complexities with a shared, cultural purpose.

This workbook series illustrates the structure of interactions with a skilled companion in any outdoor or indoor multi-sensory environment setting. MSE applications integrate a relationship-building framework (Gentle Teaching) that connects core human values with experiential learning processes that guide awareness and growth in the direction of 'feeling safe and loved," an essential, foundational value for quality of life.

MSE processes nurture self-determination and a sense of belonging by cultivating companionship, creating accessibility for the unknowable human potential for greater unity and community through experiential learning and growth.

Dr. Tony's vision for orchestrating the development of an MSE Sensory Solutions Book Series brings together the knowledge and expertise of many dedicated professionals. With consultations, collaborations, and scholarly contributions from his colleagues around the world, he engages in shared dialogue and expands on topics that illustrate steps for the training, skills, and competencies used for experiential learning in multi-sensory environments, demonstrating how communicating with *Our Tools* of presence, words, eyes, and hands is the heart of human connection and relationship-building. These connections engage a dynamic framework of sensory solutions for navigating the MSE journey.

Therapeutic, educational, and recreational goals focus on the organic engagement and intrinsically motivated exploration, movement, reflection, and reciprocation with individuals or groups. Connections, *not corrections*, cultivate and anchor the foundation of being and becoming human, capturing glimpses of the irreplaceable value and emergent meaning of human existence, inseparable from a practice of compassion for maintaining a culture of hope and for preserving a culture of gentleness.

~ ~ ~

You are invited to get more out of this book series with companion webpages for each title.

SETS of supplemental training materials are accessible for continued learning or training, using the QR code below or by visiting (https://qualityoflifeinstitute.org/mse-03-creating-meaningful-moments/)

Digital and downloadable materials include questions, exercises for competencies and proficiencies, and additional resources.

The QR code below can be used to join the SS Membership Library of the MSE Training Series.

ACKNOWLEDGEMENT

With sincere appreciation to
Katy Barrilleaux and the client services team at
RAINMAKER DIGITAL SERVICES, LLC
*for always going the extra mile
with technology support and solutions.*

HTTPS://RAINMAKERDIGITAL.COM/

Table Of Contents

1. MSE Process as a Meaningful Shared Experience — 1
2. Creating Meaningful Experiences — 6
3. The Foundation of Gentle Teaching — 12
4. Keystone for Connection — 26
5. Engaging in a Culture of Gentleness — 38
6. Purpose is Teaching the Four Pillars — 44
7. Pillar One: Feeling Safe — 52
8. Pillar Two: Feeling Loved — 58
9. Pillar Three: Being Loving — 64
10. Pillar Four: Being Engaged — 70
11. Our Tools of Gentle Teaching — 76
12. Meaningful Relationship — 88
13. Elements of Companionship — 94
14. Companionship Element 1 – Interactions — 102
15. Companionship Element 2 – Dialogue — 106
16. Companionship Element 3 – Protection — 112
17. Companionship Element 4 – Rewards — 118
18. Companionship Element 5 – Companionship — 124
19. Companionship Element 6 – Engagement — 130
20. Companionship Element 7 – Purpose — 136
21. Companionship Element 8 - Flexible Focus — 142
22. Companionship Element 9 – Memories — 148
23. Companionship Element 10 – Language — 154
24. Self-Reflection with Reference Sheet — 162
25. GIFTS – Reciprocation / Culture of Hope / Human Connection — 174

MSE PROCESS AS A MEANINGFUL SHARED EXPERIENCE

A multi-sensory environment (MSE) is an inviting, relaxing, and exploratory space, inviting intrinsic curiosity for 'true learning' [1] through the engaged, experiential processes of social-emotional development. Experiential learning especially supports and benefits individuals with various challenges and difficulties.

An MSE room (indoors or as an outdoor setting) offers engagement in **m**eaningful **s**hared **e**xperiences; MSE processes for experiential learning are facilitated by a skilled companion who mentors and builds a relationship with the individual, by valuing, protecting, teaching, and reciprocating value. Reciprocation by the Individual indicates their experienced value of what is being shared and learned together.

---

[1] McLeod, Dr. Saul. (updated 2014), Simply Psychology, Carl Rogers. https://www.simplypsychology.org/carl-rogers.html

Interactions cultivate companionship and a sense of belonging, connecting value and meaning with social-emotional awareness and growth.

Elements within the MSE environment are arranged to nurture engagement and meaningful interactions. Soft, warm lighting creates a welcoming ambiance, while comfortable seating encourages relaxation and openness. The walls are inviting with thought-provoking artwork and inspiring quotes, creating a visually stimulating atmosphere that sparks curiosity and dialogue.

The room is equipped with various interactive tools, such as plastic balls, light strings, a glow board, acoustic toys, and sensory objects that encourage creative expression and shared activities. These playful, interactive objects are tools that promote self-reflection, communication, and collaboration, inviting individuals (or others if in a group) to explore their emotions, thoughts, and experiences, together with the skilled companion.

The presence of a skilled companion in this space is instrumental in shaping the MSE experience. Whether it's a child, client, or group, the value lies in the power of and opportunity for genuine, human connection. Through active listening, empathy, and non-judgmental support, individuals in the multi-sensory environment can share their stories, struggles, and joys, feeling seen, acknowledged, and understood.

The MSE promotes a sense of being safe and trusting, empowering individuals to explore their vulnerabilities and work towards personal growth. Whether it's a child discovering their creativity, a client uncovering their inner strengths, or a group fostering mutual trust and companionship, the room invites engagement in creating meaningful moments that can positively impact lives.

Ultimately, the MSE environment celebrates the richness of human connections, encouraging individuals to form deeper bonds, gain new perspectives, and find feelings of inner contentment with shared experience, especially during times of disturbances. It is a space where personal growth flourishes, compassion thrives, and lasting memories are created.

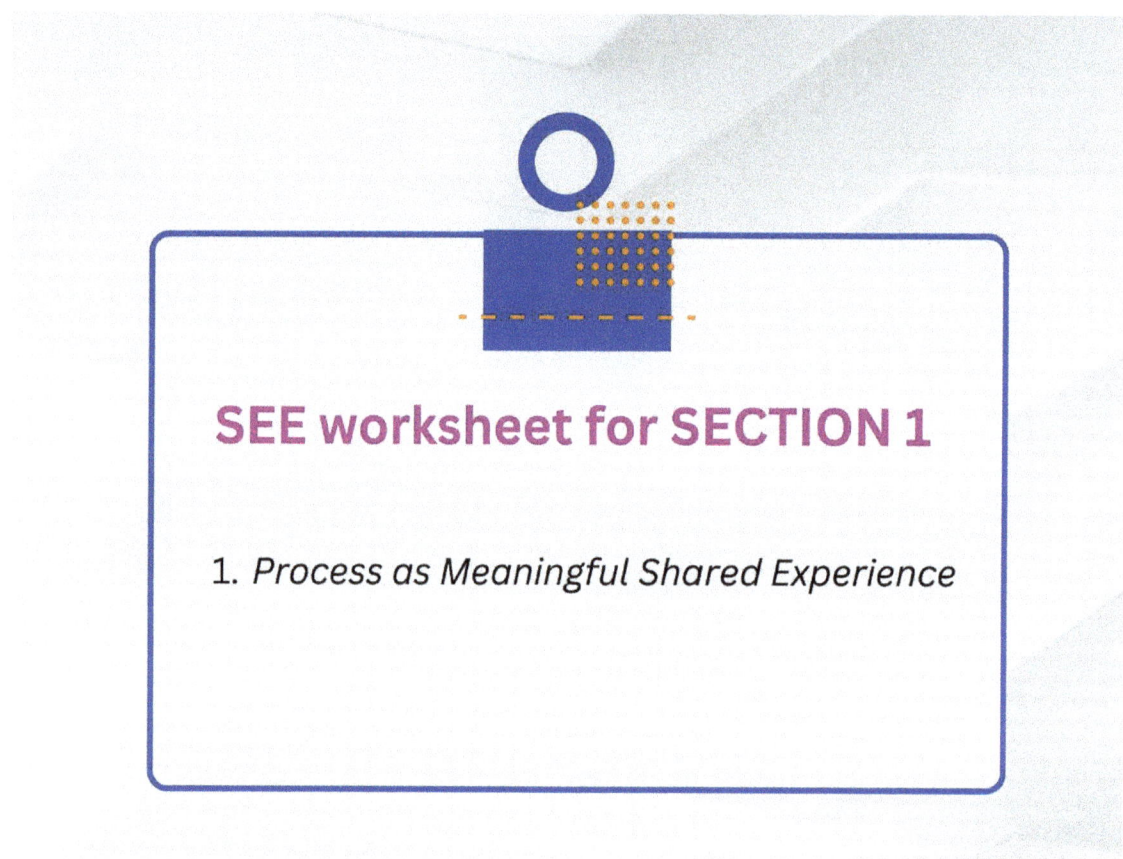

Notes:

CREATING MEANINGFUL EXPERIENCES

In the realm of human connection and personal growth, shared experiences hold immense value by expanding meaning and significance. When coupled with the presence of a skilled companion, these experiences become pronounced in social-emotional awareness and development as having meaning and value, progressing as the initial social point for change.

This section explores the significance of shared experiences in an MSE environment, and how a skilled companion can create more meaningful moments within the context of relaxation, education, and therapy; the three areas specified in the original MSE established concepts.[2]

---

[2] SEE Book 01 of this series: The Snoezelen™-MSE History and 8 Factors

When engaged, the social-emotional structure of shared experience nurtures a sense of belonging. Relationship-building supports the transformation of "self" concepts, such as confidence, self-esteem, and self-worth. When individuals engage in activities or conversations together and make meaningful connections, the shared space and connection provide an opportunity to truly understand (the emotional attunement) and be understood, promoting a sense of validation and emotional support.

A skilled companion plays a pivotal role in guiding and facilitating shared experiences within an MSE room. Expertise and an empathic presence create an unconditionally valued and safe space for individuals to explore their thoughts, feelings, and experiences. Through active listening, empathy, and effective communication, they can establish a foundation of trust that supports vulnerability and growth.

The skilled companion focuses on creating an atmosphere of calm for one's feeling of being safe and loved. Various techniques such as soothing music, aromatherapy, and guided imagery, help individuals unwind and find inner peace. By providing a non-judgmental and supportive environment, the skilled companion enables individuals to let go of stress, rejuvenate, and experience profound relaxation.

In an educational context, the skilled companion acts as a facilitator of knowledge and growth. This role designs interactive activities, provides resources, and encourages curiosity and exploration. Through shared experiences like group discussions, problem-solving tasks, or hands-on learning, the skilled companion promotes engagement, critical thinking, and the acquisition of new skills or insights. This collaborative approach ensures that learning becomes an active, meaningful process.

The therapeutic application of shared experiences in an MSE room can be particularly powerful. The skilled companion employs various MSE techniques, such as expressive arts, and role-playing or storytelling, to encourage self-reflection, emotional expression, and personal growth. By actively participating in the experience alongside the individual, the skilled companion builds a trusted connection that is foundational for the exploration of sensitive topics. Through this empathic connection, the skilled companion helps individuals in gaining insights, healing emotional wounds, and developing coping strategies.

Shared experiences within an MSE room, coupled with the presence of a skilled companion, offer immense value in terms of personal growth, compassion, and connection. Whether it is relaxation, education, or therapy, these experiences deepen meaning and accelerate transformative awareness and growth. The skilled companion's expertise, empathy, and ability to create a safe and supportive space contributes significantly to the profound impact of shared experiences. Creating the invitation for the individual to engage in meaningful interactions, the skilled companion is establishing accessible means for social-emotional development. This accessibility is often not available for people with physical and cognitive disabilities. Social-emotional human development needs relationship-building interactions. The multi-sensory environment is facilitated by the skilled companion who assists the individual in the discovery and exploration of their inner, social-emotional world, where they can be given tools that help in developing the necessary skills for social-emotional awareness and growth.

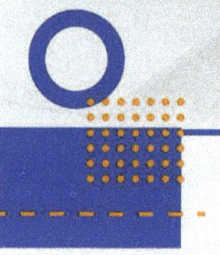

SEE worksheet for SECTION 2

2. Creating Meaningful Experiences

Notes:

THE FOUNDATION OF GENTLE TEACHING

Gentle Teaching approaches interactions, especially those involving relational support (like what we find in the MSE room), with relationship-building. Gentle Teaching establishes a relational context for human existence by cultivating a sense of belonging (companionship) and creating the invitation to experience belonging with others (community).

A basic principle of Gentle Teaching is to not let the valuing of others be contingent on conditions. Valuing without conditions (unconditional love) is practiced in addressing social-emotional barriers that tend to define existence. These barriers include feelings of isolation, disconnection with self and others, a lack of meaning for one's life, a lack of purpose or value, disorientation brought about by mental instabilities and disorders, or oppressive, abusive, or other unpredictable environments, including homelessness.[3]

A practice of Gentle Teaching cultivates a relationship dynamic for teaching and mentoring that invites interest and curiosity in learning together. In the MSE room, the skilled companion will utilize role modeling for demonstrating how to create and engage in dialogue (verbal and non-verbal). The dialogue teaches the four pillars, or four life-lessons that develop the foundation for one's learning how to feel safe, loved, loving, and engaged. A Gentle Teaching Framework gives support and accessible means to opportunities for social-emotional awareness and growth. Together, the individual, with the skilled companion, can re-imagine and re-frame self-concepts and a sense of belonging, by doing things together and engaging in the MSE processes.

A sense of belonging is mirrored in one's sense of identity, with the feeling that "I exist!"[4]

---

[3] McCROVITZ, A. (2021) Return to Gentleness, Journeying with Gentle Teaching, Outskirts Press.
[4] Ibid.

Self-perception is a main frame of reference for re-viewing the dynamic aspects of interactions, observing how we engage, feel connection, and experience coherence between the emotional (inner) and social (outer) worlds of experience. Self-concepts inform a sense of identity, deeply influencing and shaping a person's life experience. Essentially, "sensed" human experience is processed as a "feeling" experience that stems from how one is able (with awareness, tools, and skills) to interpret and perceive through the lens of value and meaning. This *in-sight* is the phenomenal and foundational social-emotional framework that is inherently human. It is this framework that *in*-forms and shapes the sensory processing center and is the narrative structuring for quality of life.

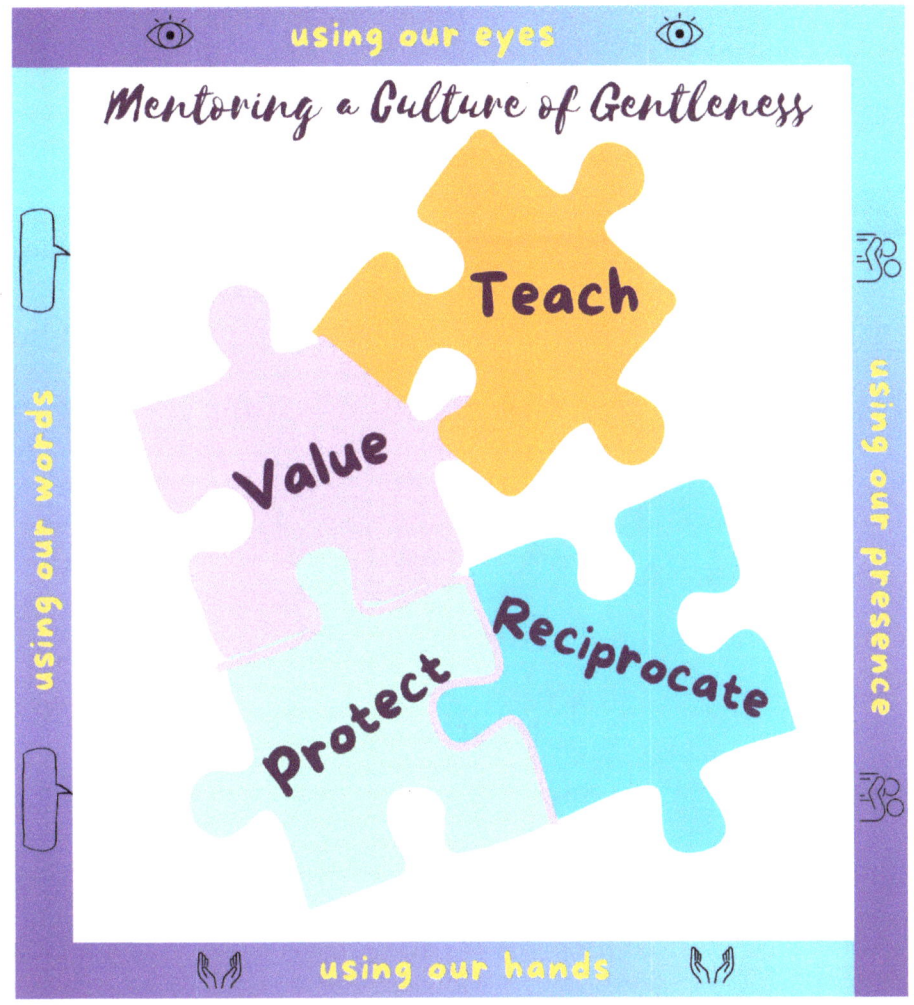

In the MSE room, valuing, teaching, protecting, and reciprocating with the individual is attributed to mentoring a culture of gentleness, and the skilled companion is in a mentoring role at all times with the individual. Even when not teaching, the skilled companion maintains the mindful mentoring of the human connection that is being sustained with how they are valuing, teaching, protecting, and reciprocating with the individual.

Value is upheld in the MSE room and in our interactions by the Four Pillars that are the life-lessons and relationship goals of feeling safe, loved, loving, and engaged. *Value* is sustained for continued growth and awareness and overall quality of life by the mentoring aspect of a Gentle Teaching framework, exploring, together, the MSE destinations. The skilled companion's active valuing of the relationship is essential. Together, with the individual's trusted engagement, the relationship dynamic navigates the course of the MSE experience. It is the vehicle for movement, inviting and guiding imagination and curiosity, prompting response, reflection, and engagement by the individual in the MSE room.

In developing human potentials, valuing cultivates receptivity and the foundation of feeling safe and loved; the port from which an individual can feel it is safe to venture on an inner journey of relationship-building, reciprocated by engagement with the outer journey of the animated self is mirrored in the motion and movement of the MSE room.

In the MSE room, the concept of teaching takes on a profound meaning, as it goes beyond traditional instruction to encompass nurturing and developing the individual's potential. The skilled companion understands that teaching begins with valuing the person and establishing a genuine human connection. Relationship-building tools are used for creating a safe and loving environment where the individual can feel secure and accepting of the invitation to explore their inner world. The trusted relationship supports and celebrates the individual's trusting step of engagement with the transformative processes for awareness and growth, and the MSE journey is set in motion.

The Four Pillars (feeling safe and loved, loving and engaged) guide this journey. Each pillar is a cornerstone in the mentoring process, ensuring that the relationship remains a source of growth, awareness, and overall quality of life. The skilled companion actively embraces and upholds these pillars, demonstrating a commitment to the individual's well-being and development.

The role of the skilled companion accounts for two aspects of 'protecting.' One is to safeguard the physical and emotional well-being of the individual, ensuring they are free from harm and fear. This protective aspect enables the individual to relax, trust, and engage in the MSE experience without inhibition.

The other aspect of 'protecting' relates to safeguarding the individual's dignity and autonomy. The skilled companion creates an environment that encourages their choices, self-expression, and active participation in shaping their MSE journey.

Reciprocation is the key to forming a mutually beneficial relationship. The skilled companion gives genuine care, understanding, and support to the individual, which is also reciprocated by their trust, engagement, and willingness to explore and grow. As the relationship dynamic evolves, both parties inspire each other to delve more deeply into the learning and growth processes, with greater imagination, curiosity, and self-discovery.

In their role of mentoring a culture of gentleness with the individual in the MSE room, valuing, teaching, protecting, and reciprocating, the skilled companion is deepening the human connection that is bridging experiential impressions with social-emotional awareness and growth. Their modeling of the relationship value that reflects the pillars of Gentle Teaching, along with their mirroring of the meaningful moments being created in the MSE room, supports movement of experiential processes and the alignment of goals for quality-of-life outcomes.

In the MSE room, the individual can find a safe space and a profound opportunity for self-expression, self-exploration, and social-emotional development. As a navigational guide, the skilled companion can mirror emotions and feelings through movement, inviting and encouraging the individual to embrace their animated self. The exercise of movement can give form and shape to the feeling sense that is the inner life and landscape, prompting potentials to unfold and flourish.

The skilled companion's valuing, teaching, protecting, and reciprocating in the MSE room gives structure and movement to mentoring processes within the experiential learning environment. This reassures continuity of the foundational trust and unconditional acceptance of the relationship that supports social-emotional awareness and growth through the collaborative, experiential discovery and learning that the MSE Room offers, remembering that 'value lies in the power of and opportunity for genuine, human connection.'

The relationship-building priority of nurturing compassionate relationships with individuals, benefits those who may have experienced trauma or have developmental, intellectual, or emotional challenges. The principles and practices of Gentle Teaching are rooted in interdependency and the belief that every person has inherent worth and dignity and should be treated with kindness, respect, and unconditional acceptance.

A Gentle Teaching practice understands that challenges reflect a person's narrative story, and therefore, positive change can only be achieved through compassionate connection rather than punishment or coercion. The purpose and gift of Gentle Teaching is cultivating an environment where one can experience feeling safe and loved, loving and engaged.

Key principles of a Gentle Teaching practice include:

Acceptance Without Conditions : Practitioners of Gentle Teaching demonstrate acceptance without conditions and non-judgmental support to individuals, regardless of their behavior or abilities. They communicate through their words, actions, and body language that the person is valued, loved, and accepted just as they are.

Building Trust: Trust is a foundational element in Gentle Teaching. Caregivers focus on developing trust by being reliable, consistent, and emotionally available. They prioritize open and honest communication, active listening, and responding to the emotional and physical needs of the individual.

A Sense of Belonging: Gentle Teaching recognizes the importance for individuals to feel a sense of belonging. Skilled companions strive to create an inclusive and supportive community where everyone feels connected, respected, and appreciated. They encourage social interactions, participation in meaningful activities, and engagement in opportunities for collaboration and shared experiences.

Teaching and Empowerment: Gentle Teaching emphasizes the importance of teaching individuals essential life skills and empowering them to become more independent and self-sufficient. Caregivers provide gentle guidance, break tasks into manageable steps, and celebrate each small achievement to promote a sense of competence and self-worth.

Emotional Regulation and Conflict Resolution: Gentle Teaching encourages individuals to develop emotional regulation skills and offers support in managing their emotions. The skilled companion models empathy, active listening, and constructive problem-solving techniques, helping individuals understand and express their emotions in healthy ways.

Gentle Teaching recognizes that the journey towards growth and healing is unique to each individual's experience, acknowledging the potential for setbacks and challenges along the way, but remaining steadfast in its commitment to model a culture of kindness, respect, and love.

Concepts of identity (ie self-perception, self-awareness, self-worth, etc.) unfold from the transparent, social-emotional, foundational fabric that is sown and shaped through human interactions. Creating a culture of gentleness in the MSE room relates to the mentoring aspects that nurture and support the individual in their engaged discovery and exploration. In relationship-building, the demonstration of valuing, teaching, protecting, and reciprocating is maintaining the trusted companionship. The movement of the relationship engages in the mending of tears and the meaningful moments that invite awareness and new moral memory to form. The mentoring processes build bridges that connect one's inner journey with the outer world of value and meaning that is expressed and represented in the MSE room.

The skilled companion cultivates a relationship based on trust, love, and engagement, validating, the individual, inviting them to engage, discover, and explore their inner, social-emotional landscape. When the individual's awareness begins to focus on their reflective, inward journey, they need to feel supported with companionship for exploring and connecting with the outer world of the MSE room, along with the expanded relationship-building that invites experiencing a sense of community.

Notes:

KEYSTONE FOR CONNECTION

Gentle Teaching is a keystone for social, emotional, and physical development, both inside and outside of the MSE room, providing the necessary foundation for individuals to experience awareness, growth, social-emotional connections, and overall well-being across various aspects of their lives.

Gentle Teaching focuses on nurturing the meaningful relationships that are essential for social development. Within the MSE room, the skilled companion builds the relationship with the framework of Gentle Teaching to create a safe and accepting environment where individuals can engage in shared experiences and develop social skills. By emphasizing unconditional acceptance, building trust, and affirming a sense of belonging, individuals feel comfortable and empowered to initiate and maintain positive social interactions. This translates beyond the MSE room when individuals begin to transfer their newly discovered social skills and confidence into their daily lives, forming authentic connections with others and participating more actively in their communities.

Emotional development is foundational to overall well-being, and Gentle Teaching places a strong emphasis on emotional regulation and self-expression. In the MSE room, individuals are encouraged to explore their emotions in a safe and supportive environment.

The principal method, or language of communication with the relationship-building framework of Gentle Teaching, is one that centers on the qualities of our presence, our words, and how we use and move our eyes and our hands, assuring trust and unconditional acceptance. These are named *Our Tools*, and Chapter 11 will talk more about the importance of how we communicate with Our Tools.

The skilled companion models compassion, active listening, and unconditional acceptance, allowing individuals to develop a deeper understanding of their own emotions and those of others. Through this emotional development within the MSE room, individuals gain the tools and self-awareness necessary for befriending their emotions in various contexts beyond the room, having increased potential and probability for healthier relationships, improved self-esteem, and greater social-emotional balance for overall well-being.

While Gentle Teaching primarily focuses on social and emotional development, it also indirectly supports one's physical sense of place and motion, body awareness, and movement.

The multisensory environment that is the MSE room, provides opportunities for individuals to engage in physical activities that promote sensory integration, coordination, and body awareness. Whether it's exploring different textures, engaging in gentle movement exercises, or interacting with sensory equipment, individuals can enhance their physical skills and sensory processing abilities. As individuals become more attuned to their bodies and gain confidence in their physical abilities within the MSE room, they may transfer these skills to other settings, leading to improved physical coordination, balance, and general motor development.

In the MSE room, the relationship-building framework of Gentle Teaching that is moving the journey of interactions and dialogue toward destinations of 'safe and loved' for social-emotional awareness and growth, expands its foundational support in navigating a physical level of dynamics that focuses on the myriad movements of the human body.

Rudolf Laban's comprehensive **movement framework** observes human movement as three-dimensional, offering insight and knowledge in this area with a comprehensive vocabulary and methodology for the observation, identification, and interpretation of movement in various contexts, including that of the MSE room.

The four components of the *Laban Movement Framework* [5] consider the basic elements of *body, effort, shape,* and *space*. This field of study emerges from basic principles and concepts that acknowledge 'movement' as a fundamental, non-verbal language of human expression and communication. Can you identify Laban's four aspects

---

[5] WAHL, C. (2019) Laban / Bartenieff Movement Studies Contemporary Applications, Human Kinetics, Champaign, **L**

of movement (body, space, effort, relationships) in the following image?

Photo Credit: From the mse collection of Lesley Rocklin, TFH Canada

Observable indicators and the modeling of applications with the Laban Movement Framework will correlate to the skilled companion's learned comprehension and understanding of 'movement' concepts and patterns, and the greater potential for expression that this offers.

MSE processes move in tandem with the companionship relationship. In this context, each element of the Laban Movement Framework is relative to the skilled companion's role and can be explored.

Body Element of Movement (What the Body Does): The body aspect refers to the specific movements and actions performed by the individual in the MSE room. A skilled companion might encourage the individual to engage in various activities that involve body movements, such as:

> Dancing: Inviting the individual to move their body rhythmically to music, expressing emotions and feelings through dance.
>
> Stretching: Encouraging gentle stretches to promote relaxation and physical well-being.
>
> Reaching: Guiding the individual to reach for objects or sensory items within the room to explore their environment actively.[6]

---

[6] Ibid

Space *Element of Movement* (Where the Body Moves): The space aspect deals with how the body moves through the physical environment of the MSE room. A skilled companion might facilitate the exploration of space in different ways:

> Locomotion: Encouraging the individual to move around the room, exploring different corners and areas to interact with the diverse sensory stimuli present.
>
> Levels: Guiding the individual to move up and down, exploring high and low positions to experience various sensations.
>
> Pathways: Suggesting specific movement paths or patterns to follow within the room, creating a structured yet engaging experience.[7]

Effort *Element of Movement* (How the Body Moves): The effort aspect of the Laban Movement Framework focuses on the qualities and dynamics of movements. The skilled companion might change the way an individual moves to promote different experiences:

---

[7] Ibid

Flowing: Encouraging smooth and continuous movements to promote a sense of calm and relaxation.

Percussive: Guiding the individual to engage in more abrupt and rhythmic movements, which can help release pent-up energy or emotions.

Lightness: Encouraging gentle, effortless movements to foster a sense of weightlessness and ease.[8]

Relationship *Element of Movement* (With Whom or What the Body Is Relating): The relationship aspect considers the interactions and connections the individual makes with others or the environment. A skilled companion has a supporting role in these relationships:

Support and Encouragement: Being an engaged presence for the individual, providing encouragement and positive support during their explorations.

---

[8] Ibid

Shared Movement: Engaging in movements with the individual, such as mirroring their actions or engaging in cooperative play, strengthens the bond of companionship.

Interaction with Sensory Stimuli: Guiding the individual to interact with sensory items in the room, fostering a relationship with the various stimuli and promoting sensory exploration.[9]

A skilled companion's understanding of the Laban Movement Framework and its applications expands the parameters of the MSE experience with increased potential for sensory solutions and quality-of-life outcomes.

The multi-sensory room that we are discussing communicates with sensory languages (ie, color, sound, touch, smells, imagery, etc.), the language of physical movement (related to 'body language'), and the language of the heart with Gentle Teaching, navigating the course of the MSE journey with value and meaning of companionship and community, with every element connecting and cultivating quality-of-life outcomes.

---

[9] Ibid

In summary, a Gentle Teaching framework is a foundational keystone for holistic development, encompassing social, emotional, and physical aspects, and can also serve as the foundational support for navigating a physical level of dynamics that focuses on the myriad movements of the human body. By creating a nurturing and accepting environment within the MSE room, skilled companions who practice Gentle Teaching empower individuals in developing essential social skills, regulating and expressing their emotions, and enhancing their physical abilities. The skills and experiences gained within the MSE room naturally extend beyond its boundaries, positively influencing individuals' social interactions, emotional well-being, and physical development in their everyday lives.

Notes:

Notes:

ENGAGING IN A CULTURE OF GENTLENESS

"Compassion is a crucial element in Gentle Teaching. Compassion is a core quality of every human being; we all have it, even if we don't always know it or show it.

Compassion has three elements. The first is the empathy to feel the suffering of others. Second is the knowledge that every human being wants to be free of suffering and also has equal rights to be free of suffering. Third is the active wish and action to help others to be happy and free of suffering.

Even if there are circumstances which make it hard or impossible to make a person happy, experiencing our compassion will be good for him. And also for us. Scientific research has shown that feeling compassion is good for our mental health as well as for our physical health.

Compassion is a very strong and unconditional energy. This energy can help us deal with challenging moments and it's the energy that teaches the other person to feel unconditionally loved by us. Without compassion there is no gentle teaching and no companionship."[10]

-Pouwel van de Siepkamp

---

[10] van de Siepkamp, P. (May 2015). Gentle Teaching Newsletter, issued by the Gentle Teaching Foundation Netherlands.

Creating meaningful moments within the MSE room is considered a privilege that benefits both the individual and those who walk with them in the culture of gentleness. This privilege lies in the transformative power of connection, compassion, and shared experiences.

For the individual, these meaningful moments offer a sense of belonging, validation, and personal growth. Within the MSE room, skilled companions and individuals engage in activities, dialogue, and sensory experiences that create deep connections. These moments allow individuals to express themselves authentically, explore their emotions, and develop a sense of self-worth. Through relationship, a path of social accessibility is established for being seen, heard, and understood. Experiencing the affirming of their value and existence expands awareness and acceptance of their own identities.

Meaningful moments envelop the permeable boundaries of the MSE room. The culture of gentleness within this space extends its influence to the outside world, shaping the way individuals navigate relationships and interactions in their everyday lives. By experiencing genuine connections and compassion within the MSE room, individuals can carry these values into their interactions with others outside of this environment. They are more likely to treat others with kindness, respect, and acceptance, creating a ripple effect of positive social change.

Skilled companions and facilitators are also privileged through the creation of meaningful moments. The opportunity to witness personal growth, self-discovery, and moments of joy in the lives of others is rewarding. These moments reaffirm our commitment to modeling a culture of gentleness that nurtures compassion and connection. Meaningful moments are a reminder of the profound impact we can have on others' lives by offering our presence, support, and understanding.

Active participation in the creating of meaningful moments contributes to a larger, cultural shift that is prioritizing authentic human connection. A culture of gentleness extends beyond the MSE room, shaping interactions with colleagues, friends, family, and others in the world community. A culture of gentleness embodies the values of empathy, respect, and acceptance, creating spaces where others can feel seen, valued, and heard.

In this way, creating meaningful moments becomes a privilege that enriches not only the lives of individuals within the MSE room, but also ourselves and the broader communities that are inevitably strengthened by our contributions to a culture of gentleness that values human connection, empathy, and personal growth.

SEE worksheet for SECTION 3

3. *The Foundation of Gentle Teaching*
4. *Keystone for Connection*
5. *Engaging in a Culture of Gentleness*

Notes:

Notes:

PURPOSE IS TEACHING THE FOUR PILLARS

Creating a Safe, Loved, Loving, and Engaging Environment

The MSE room is designed to nurture individuals with a safe, loved, loving, and engaging environment. Rooted in the principles of Gentle Teaching, the sensory stimulation and relaxation within the multisensory space promotes overall well-being, emotional regulation, and personal growth. This section explores the purpose and significance of being in the MSE room, highlighting its role in creating a safe space where individuals can feel loved, loving, and fully engaged in their sensory experiences.

1. Being and Feeling Safe:

The MSE room serves as a sanctuary where individuals can feel secure, valued, and protected. The carefully controlled environment, free from external distractions and sensory overload, fosters a sense of safety and calmness. Soft lighting, soothing music, and comforting textures create a gentle atmosphere that helps individuals relax and feel at ease. This feeling of being safe allows individuals to let go of stress and anxiety, facilitating emotional regulation and a state of inner peace.

2. Feeling Loved means feeling accepted without conditions:

Central to the purpose of the MSE room is the cultivation of unconditional love and acceptance. Skilled companions who guide individuals in this space provide a nurturing and non-judgmental presence. They offer empathy, warmth, and genuine care, creating an environment where individuals can feel genuinely loved and accepted for who they are. This unconditional love and acceptance promotes emotional well-being, self-esteem, and a sense of belonging, allowing individuals to explore and express themselves without fear of judgment.

3. Engagement and Sensory Stimulation:

The MSE room is designed to engage and stimulate the senses, providing individuals with a rich and immersive sensory experience. The room is equipped with a range of multisensory elements, such as bubble tubes, fiber-optic lights, aromatherapy, tactile surfaces, and soothing sounds. These sensory stimuli activate different parts of the brain, promoting sensory integration, exploration, and engagement. As individuals interact with the sensory elements in the room, they experience a heightened sense of awareness and connection with their surroundings. These initial steps lead to their engagement, curiosity, and joy.

4. Therapeutic and Educational Benefits:

Being in the MSE room offers various therapeutic and educational benefits that support individuals' overall well-being. The multisensory environment can help to regulate sensory processing difficulties, reduce anxiety, and promote relaxation. It can also enhance cognitive abilities, communication skills, and motor coordination. By engaging with the sensory elements and guided by a skilled companion, individuals can develop a greater awareness of their own sensory preferences and learn strategies for self-soothing and self-regulation.

5. Empowerment and Personal Growth:

Beyond the immediate therapeutic and educational benefits, the MSE room promotes empowerment and personal growth. In this environment, individuals are encouraged to make choices, express their preferences, and explore their own capabilities. Skilled companions provide gentle guidance, promoting autonomy and independence. Through meaningful interactions with the sensory elements, individuals develop self-confidence, problem-solving skills, and a sense of agency, that can extend beyond the MSE room into their daily lives.

The MSE room serves a profound purpose in creating a safe, loved, loving, and engaging environment for individuals. By fostering a sense of being safe and loved, the room becomes a sanctuary where individuals can readily reciprocate feelings of peace, relaxation, and emotional well-being as they engage with us in doing things together.

The engagement with sensory stimuli promotes exploration, joy, and enhanced sensory integration. Through the therapeutic and educational benefits and opportunities for empowerment, the MSE room becomes an organic garden for personal growth and the learning of skills. Ultimately, the purpose of being in the MSE room is to provide individuals with a holistic and meaningful experience that nurtures their emotional, sensory, and cognitive well-being.

4 PILLARS of GENTLE TEACHING
four life-lessons to learn and live by

LESSON 1: SAFE
"My friend, when you are with us, you are safe. These hands will never hurt you. These words will not put you down. These eyes will look warmly and lovingly at you."

LESSON 2: LOVED
"My friend, you are not only safe with us, you are loved. Love is unconditional!"

LESSON 3: LOVING
"Learn to be loving toward others." *Safe, loved, loving,* and *engaged* create the four cornerstones of service."

LESSON 4: ENGAGED
"Learn that it is good to be with others, to do things with others, and even to do things *for* others."

Notes:

Notes:

PILLAR ONE: FEELING SAFE

An individual with their skilled companion can experience a profound sense of being safe within the MSE room that is a space for creating a social-emotional foundation for companionship and community. Working together within this environment creates a meaningful connection between the individual and their skilled companion that ultimately enriches the individual's quality of life.

Unconditional valuing of the individual in the MSE room provides a safe space for the exploring of emotions, thoughts, and experiences. The presence of a skilled companion establishes a trusted foundation that allows the individual to feel secure in expressing themselves without fear of judgment or rejection. The skilled companion's expertise and empathy create a supportive atmosphere that encourages openness, vulnerability, and self-reflection.

Within the MSE room, individuals can engage in sensory experiences that facilitate emotional regulation and expression. The soothing sensory stimuli, such as calming lights, soft sounds, and comforting textures, help individuals relax and reduce anxiety. This supportive environment enables individuals to explore and express their emotions freely, providing a therapeutic outlet for emotional release and self-discovery. The skilled companion's presence and guidance further assist in validating and understanding these emotions, promoting emotional well-being.

The MSE room nurtures the companionship and connection between the individual and their skilled companion. Through trust, elements of companionship, and shared experiences in this multisensory space, a deep bond is formed. Active engagement by the skilled companion fosters mutual understanding and connection.

Companionship nurtures trust and the individual's experience of feeling safe and loved with the skilled companion and within the environment. The relationship-building that creates this trusted companionship dynamic creates the scaffolding of support that holds their sharing of experiences, thoughts, and concerns, leading to a deeper exploration of emotions and personal growth.

While the MSE room typically accommodates individual education, class lessons or other focused sessions, it can also serve as a platform for community building. Group therapy sessions or community events within the MSE room encourage a sense of belonging and social connection. By participating in shared experiences with others, individuals can develop a sense of community, finding support, empathy, and understanding. This shared sense of connection enriches the individual's quality of life by reducing feelings of isolation and promoting social interaction.

Feeling safe and being in the supportive environment of the MSE room, combined with the dynamic relationship between the individual and their skilled companion, creates a foundation for personal growth, emotional well-being, and improved quality of life.

Through the exploration of emotions, the development of emotional regulation skills, and the establishment of companionship and community, individuals can experience increased fulfillment, purpose, and connection. Quality of life extends and expands beyond the MSE room, influencing relationships, overall well-being, and the ability to engage in meaningful activities.

The MSE room, when utilized by an individual with their skilled companion, creates a safe and nurturing space that fosters emotional regulation, companionship, and community. This social-emotional foundation enriches the individual's quality of life by promoting self-expression, empathy, and a sense of belonging. The presence and expertise of the skilled companion plays a vital role in cultivating this environment, allowing individuals to explore their emotions, develop coping strategies, and experience meaningful connections that extend beyond the multi-sensory setting.

Notes:

Notes:

PILLAR TWO: FEELING LOVED

An individual, accompanied by their skilled companion, can experience a profound sense of love within the MSE room, cultivating one's social-emotional foundation for awareness and growth in experiencing companionship and a sense of community.

Within the MSE room, skilled companions embody the principles of unconditional acceptance and love. They create a non-judgmental atmosphere where individuals feel safe to explore and be their authentic selves. This acceptance encourages individuals to embrace their vulnerabilities, express their emotions freely, and feel genuinely loved and valued. The skilled companion's unwavering support fosters a sense of emotional security, promoting a deep connection between the individual and the skilled companion.

In the MSE room, skilled companions actively listen and validate the emotions expressed by individuals. They provide empathic responses, acknowledging and understanding the individual's feelings. This emotional validation allows individuals to feel heard, seen, and understood, reinforcing their sense of being loved. By receiving validation for their emotions, individuals develop a stronger sense of self-acceptance, self-esteem, and emotional well-being.

The MSE room provides a nurturing environment through its multisensory elements. Soft lighting, gentle sounds, comforting textures, and pleasant aromas create a soothing atmosphere that evokes feelings of warmth and care. These sensory experiences contribute to a sense of being enveloped in love, allowing individuals to relax, let go of stress, and experience a deep sense of well-being.

The MSE room is a space for building trust and creating companionship. Through shared experiences and interactions within this therapeutic environment, a strong bond is formed. The skilled companion offers genuine care, empathy, and support, fostering a trusting relationship that takes what is experienced and learned beyond the MSE room. Companionship instills individuals with a sense of belonging and connection.

The MSE room can also serve as a foundation for building a sense of community and connection. Group sessions or community events held in the MSE room facilitate social interaction and promote a shared sense of love and support. Individuals can connect with others who may have similar experiences, fostering a sense of companionship and belonging. The community built within the MSE room extends and expands beyond the MSE setting, contributing to an enriched social support network in individuals' lives.

The MSE room, when used by an individual and their skilled companion, creates a loving, nurturing environment. Acceptance without conditions cultivates emotional validation and a nurturing atmosphere, where individuals experience a deep sense of being loved and valued. This social-emotional foundation forms the basis for companionship, community, and enhanced quality of life. The connections formed within the MSE room, as well as the feelings of love and support, extend beyond the room setting, positively influencing individuals' relationships, emotional well-being, and overall satisfaction with life.

Notes:

Notes:

PILLAR THREE: BEING LOVING

With their skilled companion, an individual in the MSE room has the opportunity to cultivate self-love and extend that love to others, strengthening the social-emotional foundation for companionship and community. Through various therapeutic approaches and experiences, the MSE room facilitates the development of self-love and the capacity to share love with others.

The MSE room provides a space for individuals to become mindful of self-love and self-care. The skilled companion guides the individual in engaging with sensory experiences that promote relaxation, stress reduction, and emotional well-being. By participating in activities that bring joy, comfort, and fulfillment, individuals learn to prioritize their own needs and nurture self-love. The MSE room serves as a sanctuary where individuals can reconnect with themselves and practice acts of self-care, strengthening self-love and compassion.

Within the MSE room, skilled companions support individuals in developing emotional regulation skills and cultivating empathy. By engaging with various sensory stimuli, individuals can explore and understand their own emotions by learning to recognize and regulate their responses. Through the experiential processes, individuals develop increased self-awareness and their unknown potential for emotional intelligence, enabling their ability to extend empathy and understanding to others. The MSE room creates opportunities for individuals to practice empathy, building on their social-emotional foundation that supports the cultivating of companionship and community.

Interactions in the MSE room facilitate a deep connection between the individuals and their skilled companion. In this nurturing environment, individuals experience a sense of being seen, heard, and loved unconditionally. Through the skilled companion's empathic presence, individuals learn to value and love themselves, paving the way for meaningful connections with others. This sense of connection and companionship extends beyond the multi-sensory setting, contributing to the formation of supportive relationships and enriching one's quality of life.

The MSE room provides opportunities for individuals to express love and kindness towards themselves and others. Skilled companions encourage individuals to engage in activities that promote positive self-talk, self-affirmation, and self-compassion. Through these practices, individuals learn to treat themselves with love and kindness, fostering a healthy self-image.

The MSE room can be utilized for group sessions or community events. Here, individuals can share love, support, and kindness with others, deepening their community experience and enriching their social connections.

By nurturing self-love, empathy, and the capacity to be loving, MSE room experiences nurture and positively affect one's inherent social-emotional foundation with a sense of fulfillment, happiness, and meaningful connections with others. As individuals learn to love and care for themselves, they are better equipped to build and maintain healthy relationships-and a more satisfying life overall.

In conclusion, the MSE room, in collaboration with skilled companions, provides individuals with the opportunity to cultivate self-love and extend that love to others. Through practices of self-care, emotional regulation, and empathy, individuals develop a social-emotional foundation that fosters companionship and community. This foundation enriches one's quality of life by promoting self-acceptance, positive relationships, and a meaningful sense of well-being. The MSE room can become a transformative space where individuals learn to love and be loved, creating a ripple effect of love and kindness that leads and follows them past the door.

Notes:

Notes:

PILLAR FOUR: BEING ENGAGED

In the MSE room, individuals, with the presence and participation of their skilled companion, can actively engage with others, fostering a social emotional foundation for companionship and community that enriches their quality of life. Through shared experiences and interactions within this therapeutic environment, the MSE room creates opportunities for meaningful engagement, connection, and the development of a supportive community.

The MSE room can be utilized for group sessions or community events, providing opportunities for individuals to engage with others. Group activities, such as cooperative games, creative projects, or sensory exploration, encourage collaboration and interaction among participants. Engaging with others in the shared MSE space promotes a sense of belonging and social connection, enhancing one's quality of life through the establishment of supportive relationships.

Within the MSE room, the skilled companion facilitates communication and expression among individuals. Various sensory stimuli and guided interventions create accessibility for individuals to be able to communicate their thoughts, feelings, and preferences in verbal and non-verbal ways.

The skilled companion's role is to create a safe and inclusive space that encourages individuals to express themselves authentically, facilitating effective communication and emotional connection with others.

The MSE room can serve as a platform for inviting individuals to offer mutual support and empathy to one another. By engaging with others who may have similar experiences or challenges, individuals can develop a sense of shared understanding and connection. They can offer encouragement, validation, and empathy, creating a supportive network within the MSE community. This sense of mutual trust and companionship adds value to an individual's quality of life, with a foundation for companionship and a sense of belonging.

The MSE room serves as a space for individuals to share their experiences, insights, and knowledge with others. Through structured group discussions or informal interactions, individuals can learn from each other and gain valuable perspectives and insights. This exchange of ideas and personal narratives encourages a culture of learning, growth, and mutual enrichment. By engaging with others in this way, individuals can expand their social and emotional horizons, broadening their understanding of themselves and others.

Engagement with others in the MSE room can continue cultivating meaning and moral memory beyond the interactions. Individuals can develop meaningful connections that continue outside the MSE room, developing friendships, support networks, and a sense of community. The skills and social-emotional foundation established in the MSE room gives individuals increased confidence and ability for engaging meaningfully with others in various social contexts.

The MSE room, with the guidance of a skilled companion, creates opportunities for individuals to engage with others, improving social-emotional connections and receptivity for cultivating companionship and community.

Through group activities, communication, mutual support, sharing, and learning, individuals develop connections that enrich their quality of life. The engagement with others within the MSE room extends beyond the multi-sensory setting, promoting lasting relationships, support networks, and a sense of belonging in individuals' lives. This social engagement and community-building aspect of the MSE room contributes to enhanced social skills, emotional well-being, and a more fulfilling and meaningful quality of life.

SEE worksheet for SECTION 4

6. Purpose is Teaching the Four Pillars
7. Pillar One: Feeling Safe
8. Pillar Two: Feeling Loved
9. Pillar Three: Being Loving
10. Pillar Four: Being Engaged

Notes:

"OUR TOOLS" OF GENTLE TEACHING

In the presence of their skilled companion, individuals can actively engage with others, adding value and meaning to relationship-building (companionship and community). Shared experiences and genuine interactions within the therapeutic environment of the MSE room, enrich meaningful engagement, cultivate connections, and create community. The MSE room can be utilized for group sessions or community events, providing opportunities for individuals to engage with others.

In the MSE room, a skilled companion utilizes *Our Tools* as they are identified in a practice of Gentle Teaching: *presence, words, eyes, and hands. Our Tools* are used for building the relationship and creating the opportunities for individuals to establish a social emotional foundation for companionship and community. *Value* is demonstrated in relationship-building, using *Our Tools.*

Skilled companions use their eyes to convey empathy, warmth, and acceptance. The warmth of eye contact establishes a connection with the individual, acknowledging that they are seen and valued. Eye contact communicates understanding and attentiveness and helps in creating a safe space where individuals can be authentic in expressing themselves. The skilled companion's gaze invites trust and encourages the individual to engage in meaningful interactions, paving the way for companionship and community-building.

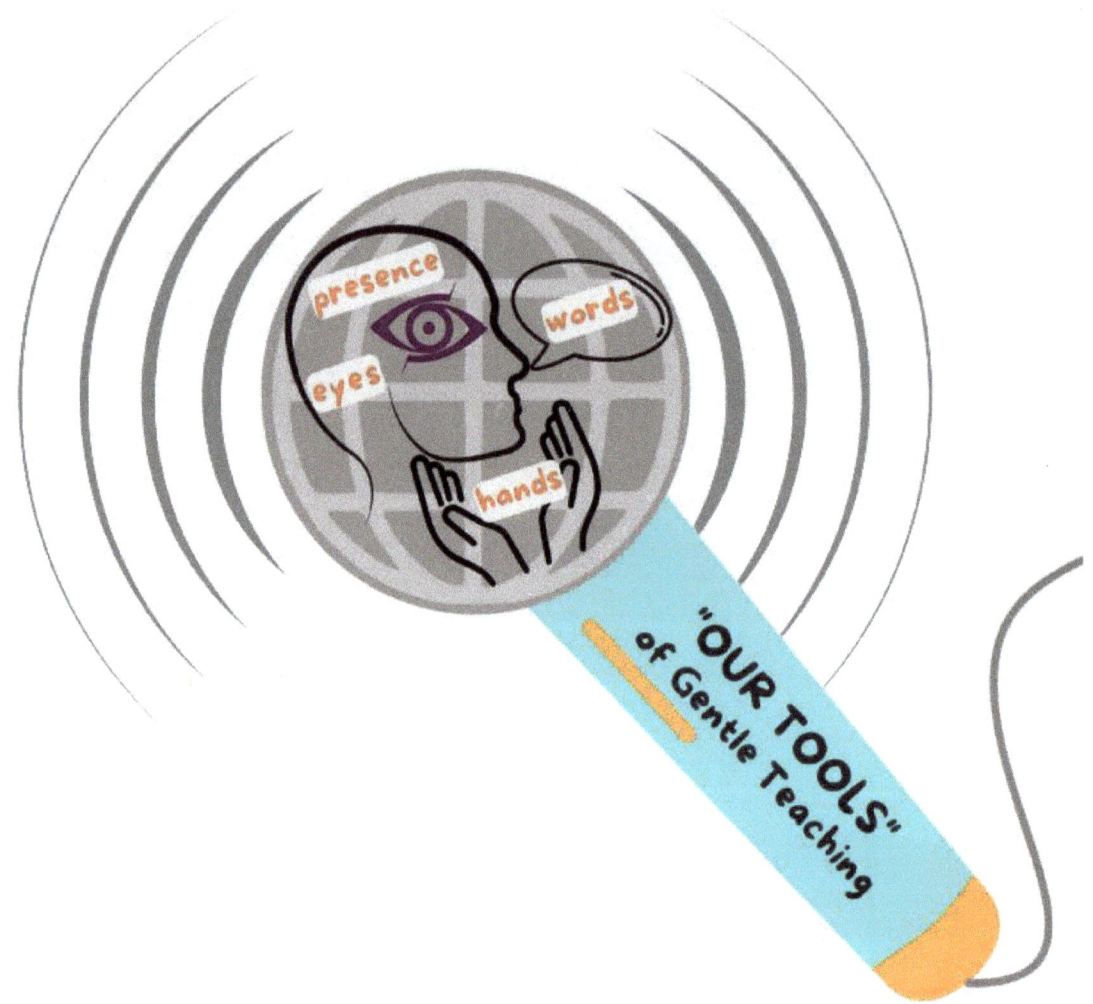

Skilled companions utilize their hands to provide comfort, support, and sensory experiences within the MSE room. They may offer gentle touches, such as a reassuring hand on the shoulder or a comforting hand-hold, to convey care and connection. Through tactile experiences, skilled companions can provide soothing sensations, tactile stimulation, or gentle massages, promoting relaxation and emotional well-being. The gentle touch of hands offers a sense of safety, trust, and companionship, maintaining the groundwork for meaningful connections.

Skilled companions use their words to communicate understanding, validation, and guidance within the MSE room. Through active listening and empathic responses, skilled companions create an atmosphere where individuals can feel heard and supported. They provide verbal validation of emotions and experiences, helping individuals gain insight and self-awareness.

Skilled companions offer words of encouragement, affirmation, and empowerment, nurturing self-esteem and a sense of belonging. The power of the skilled companion's words cultivates emotional connection, fostering companionship and community-building.

The skilled companion's presence in the MSE room is instrumental for establishing and building on the foundation for social-emotional learning. Skilled companions bring their focused attention, empathy, and genuine care to each interaction. They create a safe and non-judgmental space through their presence, allowing individuals to feel accepted and understood. The skilled companion's presence promotes a sense of emotional security, providing individuals with the freedom of authentic, self-expression and engagement in processes of meaningful connections. The presence of the skilled companion is consistent in building trust and cultivating the supportive environment.

For the skilled companion, being mindful of Our Tools and how we are communicating with our *presence, words, eyes, hands,* influences how one can feel and experience the created environment within the MSE room. Effective use of *Our Tools* encourages social interaction, emotional connection, and companionship. Through compassionate eye contact, comforting touch, empathic words and a supportive presence, the skilled companion can affect social emotional foundational development. This foundation anchors the value and meaning of social-emotional connections with the experiential learning of feeling safe and loved. Using Our Tools for building on and expanding from this foundation, helps individuals to form meaningful connections, build relationships, and embody a sense of community.

The skilled companion uses *Our Tools* for communicating with the individual, adding quality-of-life value by promoting social engagement, emotional well-being, and a deepened sense of belonging. Engaging with others in the shared space validates one's sense of belonging and social connection.

The skilled companion initiates and facilitates communication and authentic expression among individuals in the MSE room. Through various sensory stimuli and guided interventions, individuals can communicate their thoughts, feelings, and preferences in non-verbal or verbal ways. The skilled companion's role is to create a safe and inclusive space that encourages individuals to express themselves authentically, promoting effective communication and emotional connection with others. This engagement with peers and others strengthens social skills, empathy, and one's ability to form meaningful connections.

The MSE room provides a platform for individuals to express mutual support and empathy to one another. By engaging with others who may have similar experiences or challenges, individuals can develop a sense of shared understanding and connection. They can offer encouragement, validation, and empathy, creating a supportive network within the MSE community. This sense of companionship and emotional support builds on companionship and a sense of belonging.

The MSE room is an ideal space for individuals to share their experiences, insights, and knowledge with others. Through structured group discussions or informal interactions, individuals can learn from one another, gaining valuable perspectives and insights. This exchange of ideas and personal narratives permeates a culture of learning, growth, and mutual enrichment. By engaging with others in this way, individuals expand their social and emotional horizons, broadening their understanding of themselves and others.

Engagement with others in the MSE room can extend beyond the therapeutic settings. Individuals can continue to develop meaningful connections that continue beyond the MSE room, adding value to their friendships, support networks, and a sense of community. The skills and social-emotional foundation established in the MSE room experience can provide individuals with the confidence and ability to engage meaningfully with others in various social contexts.

With each guided interaction and experience, MSE room-settings can present opportunities for individuals to engage with others and experience group activities, find mutual support, and explore the connections of companionship and community through sharing and learning with peers. Engagement with others in MSE settings promotes lasting relationships and support networks. The social engagement and community-building aspects of the MSE room contribute to enhanced social skills, emotional well-being, and an overall feeling of contentment.

Value is demonstrated in relationship-building, by how we are using *Our Tools* of *presence, words, eyes,* and *hands.*

The resonant experience of human existence and interconnectedness is affirmed by feeling valued, acknowledged, and validated. Moments of being recognized and unconditionally appreciated for who we are and where we are in our own awareness and understanding, nurtures a sense of belonging and worthwhile purpose in the world around us.

Each person's individuality and unique qualities contribute to the intricate fabric of human experience. The phrase "I am because you exist" expresses the essential idea that awareness and self-concepts are shaped by human interactions. Especially in working with trauma-informed expressions, a shift in awareness evolves as new moral memory is being created and becoming rooted in the "feeling/sense" foundation of self-concepts.

Through genuine recognition and validation, a person can discover and realize that their existence is not in isolation, but in constant interplay with the world-environment and with the experiencing of human interactions. In this shared journey that cultivates the common ground of human existence, the reciprocity of valuing and of being valued promotes a profound sense of unity and acceptance that transcends the boundaries of the Self.

Gentle Teaching offers paths of accessibility to relationship-building potential with the invitational space 'between' all interconnecting points; where the mirroring of meaning and value exists for human connection; for creating new moral memory; for returning to the interdependent roots of our relational existence.

Notes:

Notes:

MEANINGFUL RELATIONSHIP

Meaningful relationships are about making connections, not corrections.

The value of creating a meaningful relationship between the individual and skilled companion in the MSE room is that this relationship dynamic is the basis for a meaningful journey that can significantly impact the individual's well-being and quality of life. Following are key aspects that highlight the value of this relationship

A meaningful relationship in the MSE room cultivates a sense of trust and safety for the individual. Trust is established through the skilled companion's consistent presence, empathic understanding, and commitment to the individual's well-being. When individuals feel safe and supported, they are more willing to explore their emotions, vulnerabilities, and challenges. This foundation of trust sets the stage for personal growth, self-reflection, and healing.

The meaningful relationship between the individual and skilled companion is a vital source of emotional support. The skilled companion provides a compassionate and non-judgmental space where individuals can openly express their thoughts, feelings, and experiences. The skilled companion's empathic listening, validation, and guidance offer individuals the support they need to navigate their emotional landscapes. The natural progression of this emotional support leads to increased self-awareness, emotional regulation, and the development of healthy coping strategies.

The MSE room provides a unique environment for individualized experiential learning and growth that can be therapeutic, recreational, or educational in nature. The meaningful relationship between the individual and skilled companion allows for a personalized approach tailored to the individual's specific needs and preferences. The skilled companion gets to know the individual on a deeper level, understanding their strengths, challenges, and goal areas. With knowledge and insight, the skilled companion can design activities, interventions, and sensory experiences that resonate with the individual, fostering a sense of connection and personal growth.

Through the meaningful relationship in the MSE room, individuals are empowered to take an active role in their own healing and personal development. The skilled companion offers guidance, collaboratively working with the individual to set goals, explore new possibilities, and overcome challenges. By fostering a sense of self-efficacy, the relationship-building connections help individuals build confidence, resilience, and a belief in their own ability to navigate life's difficulties.

The value of the meaningful relationship extends beyond the MSE room. The skilled companion serves as a consistent source of support throughout the individual's therapeutic journey, providing continuity and a safe space for exploration and growth. This long-term support contributes to the individual's overall well-being, as they have a trusted ally who can assist them in overcoming obstacles, developing coping strategies, and celebrating successes.

In summary, the value of creating a meaningful relationship in the MSE room between the individual and skilled companion is paramount. This relationship establishes trust, emotional support, and personalized care, empowering the individual to explore their emotions and overcome challenges with support. The long-term support offered by the skilled companion creates a foundation for resilience, self-efficacy, and overall well-being. The meaningful relationship formed within the MSE room can be transformative, impacting the individual's life far beyond the multi-sensory setting.

SEE worksheet for SECTION 5

11. *OUR TOOLS of Gentle Teaching*
12. *Meaningful Relationship*

Notes:

Notes:

ELEMENTS OF COMPANIONSHIP

elements of companionship...
- communicate acceptance, without conditions conveyed using our presence, words, eyes, and hands.
- create the invitation and lay the social-emotional foundation for feeling safe and loved.
- build on the foundation as we interact with the other, creating a sense of companionship and community.
- nurture the opportunity to expand and grow as new paths are made with the creating of new moral memories.

Moral memory is the social-emotional compass that is a determinant for one's outlook. Perspective and self-awareness is influenced and shaped by moral memory; how social-emotional learning is perceived, translated, and developed. Moral memory is the anchoring point of reference for experiential interpretation that predominantly initiates the sensory direction for reciprocal response and movement.

Within the MSE space of relationship-building, the individual is able, with the help of a trusted, skilled companion, to create new moral memory by connecting with a 'safe and loved' environment that becomes practical and meaningful for the centering or re-centering of one's sense of existence; of being and becoming human.

To provide an individual with opportunities through relationship-building is to ramp up accessibility to social-emotional processes that develop a sense of self and accelerate expansion in self-awareness. The companionship connection supports this naturally occurring unfoldment of greater value and new meaning for one's quality of life.

Skilled companions have the responsibility of creating a non-judgmental, 'safe and loved 'atmosphere, conveying acceptance without conditions to individuals in the MSE room. How is this type of atmosphere developed? Primarily, with our presence, and how we express value and meaning with our words, eyes, and hands. Effectively communicating with Our Tools is cultivating companionship and community and facilitating personal growth with the making of new moral memory.

Our hands can offer physical comfort, reassurance, and a sense of safety. Gentle touches, such as a comforting hand on the shoulder or a soothing hand-hold, convey empathy and care. By providing tactile experiences, such as massages or sensory stimulation, we create a space where individuals feel grounded and supported. As one of Our Tools, hands establish trust, create social-emotional connections, and nurture an individual's inherent ability to feel 'safe and loved.'

The eyes offer unconditional acceptance and empathy. Through compassionate eye contact, we communicate to others that they are seen, heard, and valued. Eye contact conveys our presence and attentiveness, making individuals feel acknowledged and validated. Maintaining a non-judgmental gaze helps in establishing a safe space and in facilitating the formation of a deep emotional bond, built on trust and love.

Our words are powerful. Choosing our words carefully and intentionally-provides verbal validation, encouragement, and support to individuals. Affirmations, empathic reflections, and kind reassurances help individuals feel understood and accepted. With our words, we are nurturing a sense of belonging and creating an environment where individuals can explore their emotions, thoughts, and experiences without fear of judgment.

Our mindful presence in the MSE room is essential for establishing a safe and loved foundation. Being fully present demonstrates commitment and dedication to the individual's well-being.

The skilled companion strives to create a space that is free from distractions. Attuned presence establishes a sense of trust and emotional security, providing the groundwork for companionship and a sense of community.

Our Tools (presence, words, eyes, hands) lay the foundation of feeling *safe and loved*, the destination for journeying together in the MSE room. Using Our Tools for integrating elements of companionship, nurtures an environment where individuals can feel supported, connected, and valued. Individuals are encouraged to engage in shared experiences, collaborative activities, and meaningful interactions, developing a sense of belonging and connection with others in the MSE room.

Multi-sensory interactions are opportunities for creating new moral memories with the individual. By engaging with compassion and empathy, positive emotional experiences make an impression on one's social-emotional foundation. New moral memories construct or reconstruct a framework for personal growth, resilience, and self-compassion, establishing a reference point for future interactions. This path and direction of new moral memory encourages individuals to expand their comfort zones, explore new possibilities, and foster their own sense of agency and empowerment.

Skilled companions in the MSE room convey acceptance without conditions, using their presence, words, eyes, and hands. These are Our Tools, the tools of Gentle Teaching that establish a 'safe and loved 'foundation for creating companionship and community. Meaningful interactions become opportunities for individuals to expand, grow, and create new moral memories. The MSE room is a therapeutic environment for relationship-building that integrates elements of companionship for creating connections that nurture awareness and growth.

Relationship-building with e*lements of companionship* is reflective of intrinsic human value and is expressive of the inherent characteristics for meaningful, human connection. Without sufficient protection for emotions or feelings, social beings can become especially vulnerable when it comes to interactions of any kind.

Companionship cultivates the journey of gentleness as a shared experience, developing a sense of trust and inviting the genuine exchange and exploration of ideas and feelings.

With the developing of companionship, one can begin to sense a direction for navigating the inner, social-emotional world. Companionship paves a path of accessibility to social-emotional awareness and growth.

Like elements of sunshine, water, and the nurturing of soil that makes a garden grow, elements of companionship cultivate connections that build from and expand one's foundation of intrinsic learning, enriching the dimension of value and meaning for quality of life.

The following chapters discuss how each element is integrated for cultivating relationship-building qualities. Each element can be considered on a spectrum ranging from *feeling connected* to *feeling disconnected.*

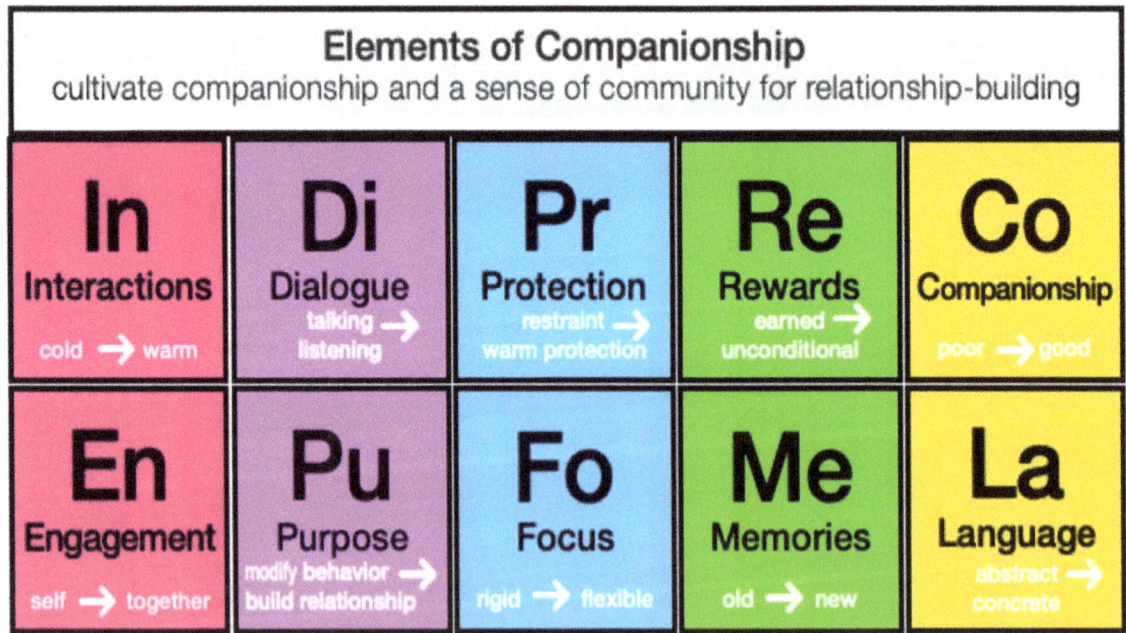

Notes:

COMPANIONSHIP ELEMENT 1: INTERACTIONS

Interactions of the skilled companion in the MSE room are warm and genuine. Using Our Tools of presence, eyes, words, and hands in a warm and compassionate manner promotes healing, connection, and growth with the meaningful moments we create together.

The tool of *presence* lays the foundation of the skilled companion's relationship-building work. Being fully present with an individual in the MSE room means being actively engaged with them, listening attentively, and demonstrating genuine interest and concern. By showing up with warmth and openness, a safe space where the individual feels valued and supported is created. Our presence conveys that we are emotionally available and committed to their well-being, assuring trust and promoting a sense of comfort and security.

Eye contact plays a significant role in establishing connection and conveying warmth in our interactions. When we meet the individual's gaze with kindness and empathy, it signals our attentiveness and deepens the sense of being seen and heard. *Our eyes* communicate acceptance, understanding, and non-judgment, allowing individuals to feel safe to express themselves authentically. Warm eye contact fosters a sense of connection and creates a space where individuals can explore their emotions and experiences with confidence.

The words we choose and the tone we use for the dialogue in our interactions influences the atmosphere within the MSE room. Warm and compassionate words create a nurturing environment where individuals can feel cared for and supported. Using gentle, affirming, and validating language validates their experiences, emotions, and efforts. Our words can provide comfort, encouragement, and reassurance, maintaining trust and emotional connection. Warmth in the words we use help to create meaningful moments, where individuals feel heard, understood, and valued.

The use of hands in a warm and nurturing manner significantly enhances the MSE experience. Gentle touches, such as a comforting hand on the shoulder or a reassuring hand-hold, convey empathy and care. Through tactile experiences like massage or sensory stimulation, we can offer a soothing and comforting presence. The warmth of our touch communicates support, safety, and compassion, helping individuals relax and feel nurtured. The tool of *our hands* is powerful for creating meaningful connections and promoting emotional well-being.

Approaching interactions with warmth and compassion, the skilled companion sets the stage for creating meaningful moments in the MSE room. Warm interactions foster a sense of safety, acceptance, and understanding, allowing individuals to lower their defenses and engage with greater ease in MSE processes. Warm interactions create an environment where individuals can feel empowered to explore their emotions, express their thoughts, and engage in learning and growth. Warm interactions invite mutual trust and facilitate the formation of deep connections between the skilled companion and the individual.

In conclusion, it is essential for the skilled companion to approach their interactions in the MSE room with warmth and compassion. By utilizing our tools of presence, eyes, words, and hands in a warm and genuine manner, meaningful moments can be created that cultivate connections and mending of the heart. These meaningful moments can evolve into transformative steps and opportunities for individuals who are exploring their emotions, building resilience, and cultivating a sense of well-being through interactions with the skilled companion in the MSE room.

Notes:

COMPANIONSHIP ELEMENT 2: DIALOGUE

Active listening by the skilled companion shapes the dialogue that centers on truly hearing and tuning in to the individual in the MSE room. Meaningful moments are made with *Our Tools* of Gentle Teaching (presence, words, eyes, hands). Active listening effectively cultivates trust, connection, and encourages engaged dialogue.

Our presence dedicates our attention and focus on the individual in the MSE room. It involves setting aside distractions and preconceived notions to create a space where the individual's voice can be heard. Our presence conveys respect, empathy, and a willingness to engage in meaningful dialogue, setting the stage for the individual to feel valued and validated, encouraging open communication.

Our eyes help in building connections for mutual understanding, reflecting, and communicating the crucial role of the skilled companion in active listening. Maintaining eye contact with the individual signals that we are fully engaged and interested in what they have to say. By looking into their eyes with warmth and attentiveness, we communicate that their words and experiences matter. It creates an environment where individuals can feel seen, heard, and understood. These are essential building blocks for creating trust and creating meaningful connections.

Our words in the MSE room are used to facilitate the individual's self-expression, rather than dominating the conversation. It is important to create a space where individuals feel comfortable sharing their thoughts, feelings, and experiences. By using open-ended questions, reflective statements, and empathic responses, individuals are encouraged to explore their insights and follow their curiosity, deepening self-awareness. Our words are used to validate the individual and their experiential learning and exploration. Our words demonstrate understanding and invite further exploration.

The tool of our hands also communicates meaningful dialogue that prioritizes listening. Instead of using our hands to impose or direct the conversation, the skilled companion uses their hands to convey empathy and support. Gentle touches, such as a reassuring hand on the arm or a comforting gesture, can communicate understanding and care. Through tactile experiences, such as hand-holding or gentle massages, the body language of our hands helps in creating a safe and calming environment that encourages individuals to relax and share their thoughts and feelings.

With the prioritizing of active listening and creating dialogue that centers and builds on the individual's experience, the individual can trust their steps toward becoming empowered as an active participant in the MSE journey with their skilled companion. Active listening allows individuals to feel valued, respected, and understood. It promotes a sense of agency and self-reflection, accelerating personal growth and a more deeply valued and meaningful self-concept. With the element of dialogue, the skilled companion uses the building of companionship to create the space and 'growing room' for the individual's experiential learning in the MSE room. The dialogue encourages self-expression and communicates that we are doing this together, creating meaningful moments that can have a lasting impression on overall well-being and quality of life.

The skilled companion prioritizes active listening in all verbal and non-verbal dialogue, avoiding talking *over* or talking *at* the individual in the MSE room. The skilled companion understands that active listening lets individuals feel heard, validated, and empowered. This dialogue supports and invites self-expression, self-reflection, and delight in self-discovery, leading to transformative experiences.

Notes:

Notes:

COMPANIONSHIP ELEMENT 3: PROTECTION

The skilled companion in the MSE room prioritizes the emotional and physical well-being of the individual. Instead of restraining or restricting an individual's actions, they strive to create a warm and protective environment that ensures safety and maintains a sense of trust. The skilled companion integrates the element of protection when using Our Tools (presence, words, eyes, hands) that communicate compassion and support. In cultivating companionship with the element of protection, the individual can feel a sense of security and empowerment as meaningful moments are being created, together, in the MSE room.

Our presence is a powerful tool used for assuring protection for the individual, not only of the physical space and supports, but of their social-emotional body of feelings and interactions. Our presence creates a warm and protective environment. When the skilled companion is fully present, they can actively assess and respond to the individual's needs, ensuring their safety and well-being. Attentiveness and responsiveness help to establish a sense of security. With this, individuals can learn that we are there to support and protect them. The meaningful presence of the skilled companion creates a protected space where individuals can feel emotionally held, guarded, and physically safe.

Our eyes convey warmth and reassurance. Maintaining gentle and compassionate eye contact communicates a sense of care and protection. Eye contact shows attentiveness and availability, assuring individuals that they are seen, protected, and supported. This non-verbal communication anchors trust in the space and in the experience as being safe and protected, physically and emotionally, within the MSE room.

Our words impart value and meaning in creating a protective environment. Comforting, reassuring, and empowering language provides individuals with a sense of emotional safety. The skilled companion acknowledges their feelings and concerns, validates their experiences, and offers support and guidance. Our words help to instill a sense of confidence and self-assurance, empowering individuals in their navigating of the MSE room and engaging in activities that promote their well-being.

Instead of restraining individuals, the tool of our hands is used for offering support, comfort, and guidance. Gentle touches can communicate care and protection, providing individuals with a sense of physical safety and protection. By using our hands to guide and assist, we help individuals move and interact throughout the MSE room, using gestures that assure safety and that encourage engagement. Our hands express emotional security for the individual. They communicate certainty and predictability—-foundational qualities of a trusted relationship for feeling safe and trusting the invitation for engagement and growth within the MSE room.

By prioritizing warm protection over restraint, the skilled companion creates an environment that promotes autonomy, dignity, and personal growth. Individuals can feel respected and supported, which allows them to explore and engage with the MSE room stimuli and activities with greater ease, in a way that is meaningful to them. This dynamic of feeling safe and empowered encourages individuals to take risks, develop resilience, and expand their comfort zones, leading to increased personal challenge and deeper connections with themselves and their environment.

The skilled companion creates a warm and protective environment in the MSE room, using Our Tools of presence, eyes, words, and hands with compassion and support. This practice prioritizes the emotional and physical well-being of the individual. Our presence and attentiveness provides a trusted sense of security. Our words offer comfort and empowerment, while our hands guide and support without restraining. By fostering a warm and protective relationship and atmosphere, the skilled companion creates meaningful moments that promote personal growth, self-discovery, and an enriching experience in the MSE room.

Notes:

Notes:

COMPANIONSHIP ELEMENT 4: REWARDS

The MSE room provides a unique space where the rewards of meaningful moments can be experienced unconditionally, without the need for the individual to earn them. The skilled companion uses Our Tools for building the relationship and creating an environment that impresses the individual with unconditional acceptance, validation, and support.

The tool of our presence in the MSE room is non-judgmental and unwavering. The skilled companion shows up with openness, empathy, and a genuine desire to connect with the individual. With our presence, the individual can feel acknowledged and that their presence and experience is valued, regardless of any participation, achievements, or expectations. Unconditional presence on the part of the skilled companion allows the individual to feel accepted right where they are and for who they are.

How will the skilled companion communicate with their eyes? This is vital for the successful conveying of this message about unconditional acceptance being 'a given, 'not something that needs to be earned. Through warm and compassionate eye contact, a sense of genuine interest, understanding, and support can be communicated. Our eyes reflect a non-judgmental stance, allowing individuals to feel seen and accepted for their unique qualities and experiences. This unconditional gaze supports an environment where the individual learns they can be authentic and vulnerable without fear of rejection.

Our words can be powerful in conveying unconditional rewards. By choosing language that is affirming, validating, and compassionate, the skilled companion creates an atmosphere of unconditional acceptance. Praise and encouragement are given, not based on performance or achievements, but on the individual's effort, progress, and personal growth. Our words become our worlds. In the MSE room, they are a source of foundational support, nurturing self-esteem and fostering a sense of worthiness, independent of external expectations.

How the skilled companion communicates with their hands can further reassure the experience of unconditional rewards. Gentle touch conveys acceptance, comfort, and care. Our hands offer support, reassurance, and a sense of safety, allowing individuals to relax and trust in the relationship-building and learning processes. Using our hands in a nurturing and non-restrictive manner communicates that the rewards of connection and support are theirs; available to them, unconditionally.

Using our tools with the intention of providing unconditional acceptance and support, helps to create an MSE space where individuals can experience the rewards of meaningful moments, without the pressure of having to earn them. This unconditional approach nurtures a sense of self-worth, self-compassion, and a sense of belonging, all of which are fundamental to personal growth and overall well-being.

The multi-sensory space with the skilled companion can be a sanctuary for an individual who can feel unrestricted in their exploration, self-expression, and self-discovery, without fear of judgment or failing conditional expectations. The MSE room is a place where the rewards of connection, companionship, and personal growth are available to each one, regardless of their abilities, achievements, or limitations. Our Tools of presence, eyes, words, and hands are used for creating a meaningful and unconditionally inclusive environment, enabling Individuals to experience the profound benefits of acceptance, inclusion, validation, and support in their journey and in their lives.

The role of a skilled companion in the MSE room is to communicate that rewards are unconditional and freely given. Our presence conveys acceptance; our eyes reflect compassion; our words are giving and affirming; our hands are nurturing. The skilled companion uses Our Tools to build the relationship, sustaining an MSE environment where individuals can experience the unconditional value and rewards of meaningful moments without the need to earn them. This inclusive and unconditional approach encourages self-acceptance, self-worth, and personal growth, expanding quality of life within and beyond the MSE room.

Notes:

Notes:

COMPANIONSHIP ELEMENT 5: COMPANIONSHIP

A primary goal for the skilled companion in the MSE room is to nurture a positive and enriching sense of companionship. With Our Tools, a multi-sensory environment can be created, cultivating a trusted and dynamic relationship with elements of companionship.

With our presence, the skilled companion is there with genuine care and interest, actively engaging with the individual. Our presence is communicating to the individual that we are there as a companion to support and connect with them. An attentive and empathic presence conveys this sense of companionship, creating the invitation for individuals to engage, share, and explore.

With the warmth and compassion of our eyes, a positive sense of companionship is communicated by the skilled companion; a connection that conveys understanding, empathy, and unconditional acceptance. Maintaining eye contact communicates to the individual that their presence is valued and that they are not alone. This also cultivates a sense of togetherness and companionship.

Our words can be used powerfully for creating a meaningful and positive sense of companionship in the MSE room. Language used by the skilled companion is uplifting, supportive, and encouraging. Affirmations, validation, and kind words cultivate companionship and understanding. With active listening, the skilled companion can respond and engage with empathy and provide a nurturing environment where the individual's thoughts, feelings, and experiences are acknowledged and valued.

Through gentle touches, comforting gestures or holding hands, a sense of connection, care, and support can be communicated. These tactile interactions promote a feeling of togetherness and companionship, creating a safe space where individuals can feel understood and valued.

Dialogue in the MSE room relates to the four pillars one is learning; to feel safe, loved, loving, and engaged. Communication is constructed with Our Tools (presence, eyes, words, and hands) in a nurturing and positive manner, so that individuals can experience a sense of companionship that is supportive, inspiring, and enriching. The discovery and exploration of companionship allows the individual to feel understood, accepted, and valued, deepening connection and trust between the skilled companion and the individual.

The solidarity one can feel with meaningful companionship in the MSE room promotes empowerment and increased engagement. The companionship element promotes a shared experience, where both the skilled companion and the individual work together towards common goals. This collaborative dynamic enhances the MSE journey and its outcomes.

The opportunity of a skilled companion in the MSE room is to create a sense of companionship that is nurturing, positive, and enriching. With Our Tools, we build the relationship, creating a dynamic that can flow easily and freely within the MSE, where the Individual feels understood, supported, and valued. Cultivating the element of companionship enhances the relationship dynamic and contributes to an overall positive and enriching experience within the MSE room.

Notes:

Notes:

COMPANIONSHIP ELEMENT 6: ENGAGEMENT

The approach of a skilled companion in the MSE room is centered around collaboration and shared experiences with the individual, rather than simply allowing the individual to roam the environment without the dynamic structure of the companionship relationship. With Our Tools (presence, eyes, words, and hands), the skilled companion creates meaningful moments by actively engaging with the individual and participating in the activities together.

The mindful presence of the skilled companion establishes a meaningful connection with a sense of togetherness. By being actively engaged and attentive, the skilled companion demonstrates their commitment to the individual's well-being and the shared experience. Our presence communicates that we are there to support and guide the individual through the activities, allowing one to experience a sense of partnership.

Our eyes establish a visual connection that conveys our interest and engagement. By maintaining eye contact and observing the individual's reactions, the skilled companion can assess their needs, preferences, and level of comfort. This visual connection helps build trust and a shared understanding, allowing the skilled companion to adapt the activities to suit unique requirements and interests.

Our words guide the shared experience in the MSE room. Both verbal and non-verbal communication explains the purpose of the activities, provides instructions, and offers encouragement. Clear and supportive language empowers the individual to actively participate and discover ways to respond and explore ways to express themselves. Our words are used to cultivate a collaborative atmosphere where ideas and feelings can be shared freely and without hesitation.

Our hands convey visual communication and support during the shared experience. The skilled companion may assist the individual in navigating the sensory elements of the MSE room, providing gentle guidance, or offering tactile stimulation as appropriate. Using our hands in a supportive and non-intrusive manner ensures that the individual feels safe, secure, and connected throughout the session.

By actively engaging with the individual and participating in the activities together, a deeper sense of connection and trust can develop. This collaborative approach allows the skilled companion to tailor the experiences to meet the individual's specific needs and preferences, enhancing the overall impact and meaning of the sessions.

Engaging in activities together also promotes social interaction and companionship by encouraging communication, cooperation, and shared enjoyment. Through active involvement, the skilled companion models and facilitates positive social interactions, helping the individual develop and strengthen their social skills.

By participating in activities with the individual, the skilled companion creates opportunities for shared joy, laughter, and emotional connection. This shared experience can elicit positive emotions and create lasting memories, contributing to a sense of fulfillment and a meaningful quality of life.

The skilled companion in the MSE room actively engages with the individual and participates in activities together to create meaningful moments. Using Our Tools establishes a collaborative and supportive environment. This approach enhances the trust and relationship-building connection, promotes social interaction, and nurtures a sense of joy and companionship. Through shared experiences, opportunities are created for the individual that support personal growth, emotional connection, and an enriched quality of life.

Notes:

Notes:

COMPANIONSHIP ELEMENT 7: PURPOSE

A primary purpose of the skilled companion in the MSE room is to build a trusted, supportive relationship with the individual, rather than predominantly focusing on modifying behaviors. With Our Tools (presence, eyes, words, hands), the skilled companion practices active listening and can hear and respond with purpose to the language and communication styles of behaviors. With a framework of Gentle Teaching, the skilled companion practices transposing what is being communicated with needed elements of companionship, reassuring and guiding the journey within a culture of gentleness.

The therapeutic dynamic of the relationship in the MSE room is not attempting to modify behavior. Elements of companionship nurture one's ability for social-emotional awareness and experiential learning, giving critical purpose to the dynamic relationship, and didactic purpose to interactions and quality-of-life outcomes.

Our presence is fundamental in establishing the trusted relationship. Being fully present means actively engaging with the individual, demonstrating genuine care, and creating a safe space where they can express themselves freely. With our presence, the skilled companion communicates to the individual that it is our privilege and purpose to be with them, letting them know we are there to listen, understand, and provide unconditional support. Our presence in the MSE room should be communicating genuine, trusted companionship, establishing the foundation for a strong alliance.

Our eyes also convey the value of the purposeful relationship and the valued time spent together, communicating empathy, and understanding. Compassionate and attentive eye contact expresses genuine interest in the individual and their experiences. Our eyes reflect a non-judgmental stance, allowing the individual to feel seen, valued, and validated; the individual can learn that each life is purposeful, regardless of abilities. Eye contact creates a connection that overrides behavior modification and encourages the direction of open communication and emotional connection.

The skilled companion uses words that are purposeful, relating to the MSE goals. Our words are meaningful. They cultivate the social-emotional foundational goals of learning the four pillars (feeling safe, feeling loved, becoming engaged and being loving). The empathic and supportive language of the skilled companion conveys their willingness to listen and validate the individual's thoughts and feelings. The skilled companion actively engages in dialogue and practices active listening.

Our hands can convey care, comfort, and support, further strengthening the purpose and value of the relationship between the skilled companion and the individual. Through gentle touch and comforting gestures, the skilled companion communicates empathy and understanding. Our hands offer reassurance, a sense of safety, and non-verbal support. By using our hands in a respectful and nurturing manner, we create an environment where the individual feels valued, respected, and cared for.

The purpose of prioritizing the building of a companion-relationship is to acknowledge the individual's unique needs, experiences, and emotions. Our purpose drives our focus, which is not to modify behavior, but to focus on discovering and understanding the underlying factors that contribute to what is being communicated through the language of emotion and the flow of movements that we tend to solidify as 'behavior.'

The purpose of the skilled companion is to work collaboratively with the individual in learning, together, how to befriend emotions and navigate toward personal awareness and empowerment in self-regulation and social-emotional development.

The purpose of a trusted and meaningful relationship is for individuals to feel supported, validated, and understood. This empowers them to explore their emotions, develop self-awareness, and make positive changes that begin from within. A safe and trusted relationship in the multi-sensory space encourages the individual to engage in self-reflection, personal and purposeful growth, and the development of coping strategies that are valued and meaningful for them.

The purpose of a skilled companion in the MSE room is to collaborate with the individual in building a trusted, meaningful relationship, then guiding the purposeful navigation, based on the individual's responses and preferences. With our tools of presence, eyes, words, and hands, the skilled companion creates meaningful moments that make connections, build trust, and communicate understanding. This approach overrides behavior modification and focuses on cultivating a strong alliance that supports the individual's emotional well-being and personal growth.

Notes:

COMPANIONSHIP ELEMENT 8: FLEXIBILITY OF FOCUS

When the skilled companion is working with the individual and building the relationship, a flexible focus, rather than one of rigidity, is essential. Our Tools (presence, eyes, words, hands) construct and engage the dialogue, creating meaningful moments that adapt to the individual's unique needs and preferences, cultivating a therapeutic environment that is responsive and supportive.

Our presence should be flexible in adapting to the individual's changing emotions, behaviors, and communication styles. The skilled companion can be attuned to the movements and communicative cues that can signal the need to adjust the process and flow of communication accordingly. This flexibility is most conducive to creating a safe and comfortable space where the individual can experience being understood and unconditionally accepted, regardless of their level of engagement or how they might feel from moment-to-moment.

Flexibility in our gaze means being receptive to the individual's visual preferences and sensitivities. Some individuals may prefer direct eye contact, while others may find it overwhelming. By being observant and responsive, the skilled companion can adjust their eye contact to respect and attune to the comfort level of the individual, ensuring that interactions in the MSE room are supporting their specific needs.

Flexibility in our language means adapting our communication style to meet the individual's abilities and preferences. The skilled companion should use clear and concise language, and consider alternative methods of communication, such as visual aids or gestures, for individuals with limited verbal skills. By being flexible in our words, the skilled companion ensures that communicated messages can be grasped and are accessible and meaningful to the individual.

Flexibility in our use of hands involves being adaptable in physical aspects of MSE interactions. When using touch or gestures, it is recommended that the skilled companion initially becomes sensitive to the individual's comfort levels and boundaries. Some individuals may prefer a lighter touch, while others may respond better to deep pressure. By being flexible in how our hands are used for communicating, we can create a therapeutic, educational, or recreational environment that respects and accommodates the individual's needs.

By adopting a flexible focus in their approach, the skilled companion acknowledges and honors the individual's autonomy and respects their choices and ability to act. Recognizing that each one is unique, with different preferences and sensitivities, methods can be adjusted accordingly, to maintain a comfortable and supportive space.

With flexibility in our focus, the skilled companion can respond in real-time to the individual's changing needs and emotional states. Flexibility allows for adaptability for shifting emotions, changing environments and activities, and allows the skilled companion to create meaningful moments that align with the current abilities and fluctuating interests of the individual. This flexibility promotes a sense of empowerment and engagement, as the individual feels that their needs are heard and respected.

Additionally, being flexible in our practice as a skilled companion allows us to foster a collaborative relationship with the individual. By co-creating experiences, navigating the course and making adjustments based on feedback, we can ensure that the individual has an active role in shaping their companionship journey. This collaborative approach encourages a sense of ownership and self-determination, leading to increased motivation, participation, and overall satisfaction.

As a skilled companion in the MSE room, it is important to maintain a focus on flexibility rather than rigidity. By utilizing Our Tools of presence, eyes, words, and hands in a flexible manner, meaningful moments can be created that adapt to the individual's unique needs and preferences. This flexibility allows the skilled companion to provide a multi-sensory environment that is responsive, supportive, and empowering. Flexibility in our focus supports the individual in feeling heard, respected, and choosing to stay actively engaged in the MSE journey with their skilled companion, ultimately enriching their well-being and overall quality of life.

Notes:

COMPANIONSHIP ELEMENT 9: MEMORIES

As a skilled companion, we have some knowledge of the individual's memories, especially those involving trauma, but we are also focusing now on creating new moral memories with the individual. Our Tools (presence, eyes, words, hands) communicate and facilitate the creating of meaningful moments that lean toward new moral memory, by shaping positive experiences, and mending tears in the social-emotional fabric as they become apparent through the interactions of relationship-building.

Our presence plays a vital role in creating new moral memories. Being fully present in the moment with the individual, the skilled companion can create an atmosphere of safety, acceptance, and support. The skilled companion's consistent and compassionate presence establishes a foundation for positive experiences to unfold and allows the individual to feel valued and understood.

Our eyes reflect a focus on the present moment, fostering a sense of connection that builds a bridge to new moral memories, based on shared positive interactions.

Our words are powerful tools for shaping new moral memories. By using affirming and empowering language, the skilled companion helps the individual reframe their experiences and develop a positive self-perception.

The skilled companion offers praise, support, and guidance, emphasizing the individual's strengths and encouraging engagement in activities that promote personal growth. Through our words, the skilled companion creates a narrative of mending brokenness and navigating the heart with possibilities that inspire new moral memories.

Our hands provide physical support and comfort, helping to create positive sensory experiences. By using gentle touch and nurturing gestures, the skilled companion can convey care and safety. Our hands can guide the individual through activities, offering reassurance and promoting a sense of connection. Through these tactile interactions, new moral memories can develop that cultivate positive associations with touch and human connection.

By focusing on creating new moral memories, the skilled companion offers the individual an opportunity to re-form their narrative and build a more positive self-concept. The skilled companion helps the individual develop a sense of agency, resilience, and self-compassion. This approach allows for growth and healing and invites possibilities for transforming past experiences into renewable sources of strength and wisdom.

While acknowledging and addressing old memories and experiences is important, the focus for the skilled companion is to provide a nurturing and supportive environment that fosters the creation of new, positive memories. By doing so, the skilled companion assists the individual in rewriting their narrative, emphasizing their strengths, and creating a culture of a sense of hope and possibility. With new moral memories being sown, creating meaningful moments looks at present and future possibilities, no longer limited by the brokenness and isolation of unresolved past experiences.

A skilled companion acknowledges the individual's history and present moral memory, but can create new moral memories. With presence, the skilled companion is empathic, uses affirming language, and provides nurturing touch. In consideration of trauma-informed memories, the skilled companion can create an environment that promotes personal growth and positive experiences that cultivate new moral memory. Through the creation of new moral memories, the individual can become empowered in the re-forming of their narrative, enriching their overall well-being and quality-of-life outcomes.

Notes:

Notes:

COMPANIONSHIP ELEMENT 10: LANGUAGE

A skilled companion in the MSE room, understands the importance of using their presence, eyes, words, and hands for communicating, and using language (verbal and non-verbal) that is concrete rather than abstract. Creating meaningful moments with the individual can unfold most naturally with concrete language that is specific and clarifying.

Our presence sets the stage for effective communication. The skilled companion focuses on how the individual is sensing and feeling, learning their needs and preferences. The skilled companion can identify how the individual is processing the stimuli by observing his interaction and movement as "moving into," "away from," or "somewhere in the middle." The attentive presence of the skilled companion reassures a safe space for open communication and supports a mutually beneficial relationship dynamic to be maintained for meaningful interactions.

Interactions in a multi-sensory environment that apply a framework of Gentle Teaching, fortify the mentoring relationship connection that is valuing, teaching, protecting, and reciprocating individuals' responses to sensory experiences.

The skilled companion values the Individual's unique responses to sensory stimuli. Whether they *move in*, *move away*, or *find a middle ground*, these reactions are all valid expressions of emotions and perceptions. By valuing their responses, the skilled companion is non-judgmental of movement ability and development. As the MSE experience expands, role-modeling might be used to introduce additional movement choices that correlate to one's individuality, expanding their options.

With a practice of Gentle Teaching, individuals can learn how to engage with the sensory environment in ways that value their preferences and comfort levels. For those who choose to move into the feeling or experience of excitement, the skilled companion encourages their exploration, supporting their personal growth with expanded perceptions.

The skilled companion guides the MSE journey that supports the Individual in embracing change and new experiences as they discover the delights of the MSE room. For individuals who feel overwhelmed and choose to move away, the skilled companion protects their emotional well-being by providing a familiar, less stimulating space. The work and presence of the skilled companion creates a safe and trusted haven for self-preservation, with the understanding that *retreat* is a coping mechanism for processing intense feelings.

The skilled companion supports those who respond with a balanced approach, finding the middle ground by teaching the individual how to assess their sensory input gradually, and at their own pace, helping them to achieve a harmonious equilibrium in their experiences.

Understanding that individual responses can vary based on context and emotional state, the skilled companion adapts interactions to the specific needs of each person. The skilled companion reciprocates their engagement by tailoring the MSE experience to suit their preferences, creating valued connections for a meaningful journey.

The MSE room embodies the principles of Gentle Teaching by valuing the uniqueness of individuals, teaching each one how to engage with the sensory environment, protecting their emotional well-being, and reciprocating their responses with care and personalized attention. This approach fosters a supportive and inclusive environment for individuals to explore their feelings and experiences, creating meaningful moments that enrich quality of life.

Our eyes speak a non-verbal language, communicating without words. Maintaining eye contact maintains a connection that communicates the interest of the skilled companion. When using concrete language, our eyes can provide visual cues that strengthen and promote understanding. We can use visual prompts or gestures to support the non-verbal communication of our eyes, helping to illustrate concrete concepts.

In our verbal communication, using concrete language means our words are specific, clear, and concise. Vague and abstract terms are avoided. Instead, the skilled companion provides tangible and specific information that the individual can relate to and readily grasp. Concrete language helps to eliminate confusion. The consistent communication with *Our Tools* (presence, words, eyes, hands) builds upon and expands the social-emotional foundation that is connecting the individual's experience to the four pillars (feeling safe, feeling loved, being loving, becoming engaged). The uninterrupted process of relationship-building supports the integration of these life-lessons, rendering one's ability for awareness and growth receptive to experiential learning in the MSE room. We can use descriptive words, provide step-by-step instructions, and offer examples to facilitate comprehension and engagement.

The skilled companion uses concrete gestures and demonstrations with their hands, physically showing the individual what we are communicating, like how to brush teeth or pour a glass of water. Concrete gestures and language enable better understanding and clarify the message. Concrete gestures, such as how we touch another's hand, communicating support from beneath their hand that is held by ours, communicates that we are doing things together, and not the skilled companion having power 'over' the individual. Simple demonstrations can make information more accessible and relatable, like 'in five minutes we will do another activity' can be demonstrated by showing them a clock and where the hands will be when it is time to go to the next step.

Concrete language supports the individual's ability to understand and engage in meaningful moments. Concrete language provides clarity, reduces ambiguity, and helps individuals make connections between their experiences and the information being conveyed. It promotes active participation, problem-solving, and empowerment.

The use of concrete language is particularly beneficial for individuals with cognitive or language impairments who may have even greater difficulty processing abstract concepts. By using clear and specific language, we meet them at their level of understanding, encouraging effective communication and meaningful interactions.

A skilled companion in the MSE room recognizes the importance of using concrete language to create meaningful moments. Using our tools of presence, eyes, words, and hands, can ensure that our communication is specific, clear, and accessible, with concrete language.

SEE worksheet for SECTION 6

13. Elements of Companionship
14. Companionship Element 1 - Interactions
15. Companionship Element 2 - Dialogue
16. Companionship Element 3 - Protection
17. Companionship Element 4 - Rewards
18. Companionship Element 5 - Companionship
19. Companionship Element 6 - Engagement
20. Companionship Element 7 - Purpose
21. Companionship Element 8 – Flexible Focus
22. Companionship Element 9 - Memories
23. Companionship Element 10 - Language

Notes:

SELF-REFLECTING IN THE MSE ROOM (WITH REFERENCE SHEET)

Self-reflection by the skilled companion in the MSE room is essential for quality-of-life outcomes. Self-reflection is an important part of any practice that involves mentoring, teaching, or interacting with others in facilitating experiential learning. Self-assessing and self-reflecting on levels and skills of engagement in the MSE processes allows the skilled companion to increase competence and continued learning as a professional.

Growing in self-awareness can shed light on our own prejudices and assumptions as they rise to the reflective surface, inviting a clearer understanding and broader perspective. Practicing self-awareness and actively reflecting on how we, as a skilled companion, are using our presence, eyes, words, hands, can provide navigational insights that support teaching goals and that also add value to interactions with a deeper level of engagement on our part.

Self-reflection exercises guide the skilled companion in examining the impression of 'our presence' with the individual and in the multi-sensory environment. We can ask ourselves questions such as: *Am I fully present and attentive to the individual's needs? Am I projecting a calm and unconditionally supportive presence?* By reflecting on our presence, we can become aware of distractions or personal biases that may be hindering our ability to connect with the individual. Increasing self-awareness leads to more effective engagement.

Self-reflection helps us examine our gaze and eye contact during interactions. We can reflect on whether our eye contact is inviting and empathic or if it conveys discomfort or judgment. By being aware of our eye contact patterns, we can focus on using our eyes to convey warmth, acceptance, and genuine interest in the individual. Self-reflection allows us to adjust our gaze and create a safe space for creating connections and meaningful communication.

Reflecting on how we use our words is essential for building trust and effective communication. Self-reflection helps us become aware of language choices, tone of voice, and the potential impact our words might be making, and whether we are using words that are respectful, inclusive, and affirming. By reflecting on our language, we can replace language with words that have value for promoting understanding and meaning for the individual.

Self-reflection encourages us to examine how we are communicating with our hands. The skilled companion can reflect on the intention preceding their touch, gestures, and physical guidance. Are hand movements conveying comfort, support, and safety? Are we respecting personal boundaries and consent? Self-awareness of what is being communicated with our hands helps to ensure that physical interactions promote a sense of trust, respect, and meaningful connection.

Self-reflection goes beyond reviewing how we are using Our Tools. It involves examining our beliefs that may influence body language and our approach to interactions. Self-reflection can help us become aware of preconceived notions or judgments we may hold, allowing us to approach each interaction with increased openness, curiosity, and cultural sensitivity.

Self-reflection and self-awareness are integral to a professional practice and add value to personal development. Competence in creating meaningful interactions is improved as we continue refining our skills, deepening our understanding of the individual's unique needs, and cultivating the relationship dynamic. It also helps us recognize and address any countertransference or personal issues that may arise during sessions, ensuring that a client-centered focus is maintained, and the individual's well-being is prioritized.

Self-reflection is an integral part of being a skilled companion in the MSE room. It enables processes of self-awareness to be understood in how we are using Our Tools and adds value and meaning to our interactions. The skilled companion continually strives to build on and expand their relationship-building skills, with self-reflection exercises that challenge assumptions and increase competence for creating value and quality-of-life outcomes with a meaningful and effective, relationship dynamic.

REFERENCE SHEET FOR SELF-REFLECTION EXERCISES

Self-reflection plays a vital role in a skilled companion's ability to be aware of how they enrich the relationship. In the MSE room, we look at four areas of a meaningful relationship. The theory and concept of interactions focusing on four particular domains was formulated by Phyllis Booth (Theraplay™),[11] who discovered that, in meaningful relationships that create an active, emotional connection (ie the parent-child relationship), four essential qualities are present. These four areas are: *structuring, engaging, challenging,* and *nurturing*. By engaging in self-reflection, the skilled companion can evaluate their approach, identify areas of strength or those that can be improved, and add value to interactions by observing and developing these four areas

---

[11] Booth, P., A. Jernberg (2010) Theraplay: Helping Parents and Children Build Better Relationships Through Attachment-Based Play. Jossey-Bass.

of relationship-building that cultivate connections and create meaningful moments.

Structuring: Self-reflection encourages the skilled companion to assess their ability in providing a structured and organized environment in the MSE room. It involves reflecting on how well they establish clear boundaries, routines, and expectations that create a sense of safety and predictability for the individual. The skilled companion can ask themselves questions such as:

Am I providing a structured space where the individual feels secure and can engage in activities with a clear framework?

Do I effectively communicate the purpose and expectations of each session?

Through self-reflection, the skilled companion can refine their structuring skills, ensuring that the individual feels supported and guided throughout their MSE experience.

Engaging: Self-reflection supports the skilled companion in evaluating their competence for engaging with individuals in the MSE room. It involves considering how well the individual's attention is captured, how their interest is maintained, and how a sense of connection and involvement is created. The skilled companion can reflect on their own presence, energy, and enthusiasm during sessions. They can ask themselves: Am I actively engaging the individual through meaningful activities and interactions? Am I adapting my approach to the individual's preferences and needs? Self-reflection helps the skilled companion identify ways to enhance their engagement skills, producing a more meaningful and interactive relationship with the individual.

Challenging: Self-reflection guides the skilled companion as they assess their approach to providing challenge for individuals in the MSE room. It involves considering how they support individuals in exploring new experiences, developing skills, and overcoming obstacles. The skilled companion can reflect on their ability to set appropriate goals, provide appropriate levels of challenge, and facilitate growth and development. Am I offering opportunities for the individual to step out of their comfort zone and expand their abilities? Am I providing the necessary support and encouragement during moments of challenge? Self-reflection helps the skilled companion identify ways to effectively balance support and challenge, ensuring that the individual's growth is nurtured within the MSE environment.

Nurturing: Self-reflection by the skilled companion is necessary for evaluating the effectiveness of their efforts in creating a supporting atmosphere that cultivates quality-of life outcomes. It involves considering how they demonstrate empathy, compassion, and care for the individual's emotional well-being. The skilled companion can reflect on their own responses to the individual's emotions, their ability to provide comfort and validation, and their approach to building trust and rapport. Am I attuned to the individual's emotional needs and responsive to their cues? Do I create a safe and non-judgmental space where the individual feels valued and supported? Self-reflection guides the skilled companion in nurturing the relationship dynamic, ensuring that the individual feels seen, heard, and understood within the MSE environment.

By engaging in exercises of self-reflection, the skilled companion can become more aware of their strengths and areas of need for growth within the four areas of a meaningful relationship in the MSE room. The skilled companion's exercises in self-awareness in the MSE room refines skills and competencies, benefiting the multi-sensory experience for the individual.

SEE worksheet for SECTION 7

24. Self-Reflection with Reference Sheet

Notes:

GIFTS
*RECIPROCATION
*A CULTURE OF HOPE
*HUMAN CONNECTION

RECIPROCATION

Becoming aware of an individual's ability to reciprocate the value of interactions and our teaching in the MSE room, will help to facilitate meaningful moments and create learning experiences with quality-of-life outcomes. By observing how an individual uses their own tools of presence, eyes, words, and hands, the skilled companion can tailor their teaching methods, adapt the environment, and provide opportunities for them to engage in creating meaningful moments.

Notice and identify what the individual is communicating with their presence. Levels of participation and engagement in the activities can quickly indicate their degree of interest. Monitor the quality of attentiveness and notice how an individual appears to be present in the moment. By learning what the individual is communicating with their presence, the teaching approach can be adjusted to match or challenge their level of engagement.

Observing how an individual is communicating with their eyes will indicate degrees of visual focus, attention, and perception. Some individuals may have a strong visual orientation, while others may rely more on tactile or auditory cues. Being aware of an individual's visual engagement helps the skilled companion in selecting visual elements, cues, or prompts that resonate with their learning style.

Paying attention to how an individual is communicating with their use of words, verbalizations, body language, gestures, movements, and other communication methods, helps the skilled companion in learning more specifically about the individual's capacity for expressing thoughts, needs, and preferences. Some individuals may have limited verbal abilities, while others may communicate effectively through augmentative and alternative communication (AAC) systems or non-verbal cues. By being aware of their communication tools, teaching methods can be adapted to ensure effective communication and meaningful learning experiences.

Observing how an individual uses their hands can reveal insight into their motor skills, exploration, and interaction with the environment. Some individuals may be more tactile or kinesthetic learners, relying on touch, manipulation, or exploration of objects to understand concepts. By recognizing their hand movements, the skilled companion can provide appropriate sensory materials, tactile experiences, or physical guidance for creating more meaningful interactions and outcomes.

Observing how an individual is using their communication tools is helpful to the skilled companion for discerning what is needed for creating a supportive environment that encourages active participation and self-expression. A safe and non-judgmental atmosphere promotes autonomy, self-confidence, and a willingness to explore and learn.

Skilled companions can also use various assessment tools, observation strategies, or collaborative approaches to better understand an individual's learning style, preferences, and progress. As a skilled companion becomes knowledgeable about an individual's abilities and utilizes their strengths, an environment can be created that acknowledges their gifts, respects their learning style, and encourages reciprocation of the value of the collaborative teaching.

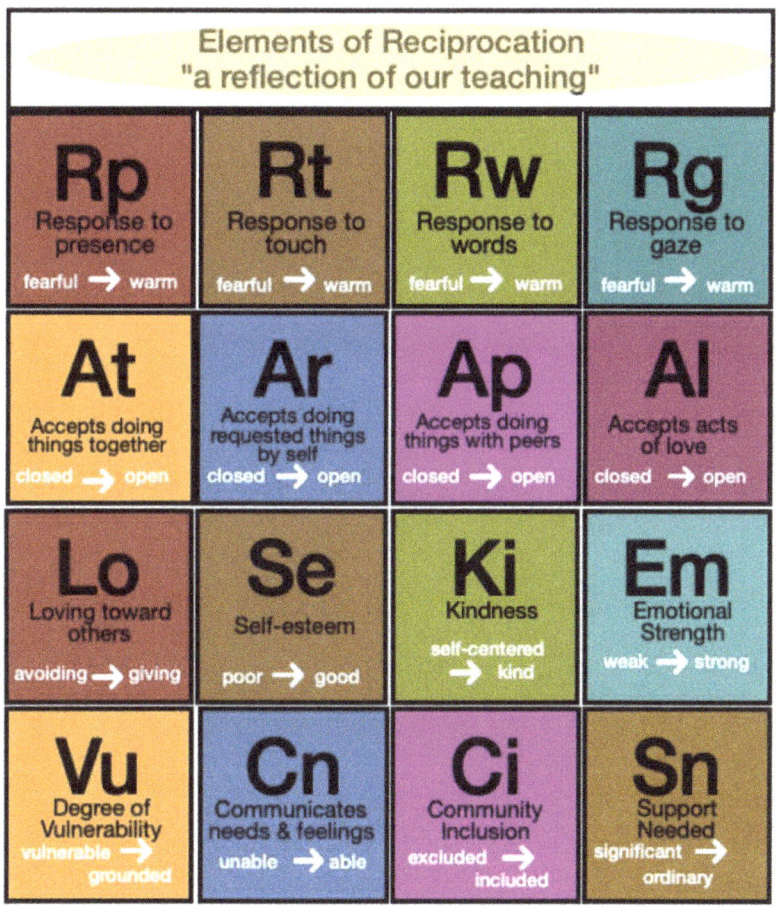

The following examples are common responses by individuals using their own tools of presence, words, eyes, and hands. Illustrate how each response relates to each of the 16 *elements of reciprocation*:

1. *Response to the presence of skilled companion*: By being aware of whether the individual responds with fear or warmth to our presence, we can adjust our approach accordingly. If they display fear, we can focus on building trust and creating a safe environment. If they respond warmly, we can build on a sense of comfort and connection.

2. *Response to touch*: Being attentive to how the individual responds to touch (with fear or warmth), allows us to provide appropriate tactile experiences. If they are fearful, we can introduce touch gradually, respecting their boundaries. If they respond warmly, we can use touch as a means of comfort and communication.

3. *Response to how words are used by the skilled companion*: Understanding whether the individual responds to our words with fear or warmth helps us adapt our communication style. If they display fear, we can use gentle and reassuring language. If they respond

warmly, we can engage in meaningful conversations and provide concrete instructions.

4. *Response to the gaze of the skilled companion*: Observing whether the individual responds to our gaze with fear or warmth indicates their level of comfort and trust. If they display fear, we can maintain gentle eye contact to gradually build a connection. If they respond warmly, we can establish a sense of mutual understanding and engagement through eye contact.

5. *Accepts doing things with the skilled companion*: Being aware of whether the individual rejects or desires doing things with us allows us to respect their autonomy. If they express rejection, we can provide choices and opportunities for collaboration. If they desire companionship, we can engage in shared activities to cultivate a sense of connection.

6. *Accepts doing requested things on their own*: Understanding whether the individual rejects or agrees to do things independently helps us support their autonomy. If they reject, we can provide

guidance and encouragement to gradually build their confidence. If they agree, we can foster independence and self-efficacy.

7. *Accepts doing things with peers:* Observing whether the individual rejects or desires doing things with peers informs our approach to social interactions. If they reject, we can facilitate gradual exposure to peer interactions and create a supportive environment. If they desire companionship, we can encourage and facilitate social engagement to promote a sense of belonging.

8. *Accepts acts of love*: Being aware of whether the individual rejects or desires acts of love allows us to nurture their emotional well-being. If they reject, we can create a safe space to explore and express emotions. If they desire acts of love, we can provide affection, validation, and emotional support.

9. *Expresses love toward others*: Observing whether the individual avoids or expresses love toward others helps us understand their social-emotional dynamics. If they avoid, we can create opportunities for emotional expression and foster empathy. If they are giving of love,

we can encourage and support their positive interactions, promoting a sense of compassion and connectedness.

10. *Self-esteem*: Understanding whether the individual's self-esteem is poor or good guides our approach to building their confidence and self-worth. If their self-esteem is poor, we can provide praise, encouragement, and activities that celebrate their strengths. If their self-esteem is good, we can nurture their self-confidence and promote further growth.

11. *Kindness*: Observing if the individual's engagement and interactions are being self-centered or kind will help the skilled companion facilitate meaningful movement, modeling how one can use their presence, eyes, words, and hands. If they are self-centered, activities can be introduced that promote empathy and perspective-taking. If they already demonstrate kindness, this can be supported by acknowledging and encouraging their acts of kindness, cultivating a sense of compassion.

12. *Emotional strength*: Observing whether the individual's emotional strength is weak or strong informs our support for emotional regulation and resilience. If their emotional strength is weak, we can provide coping strategies, emotional validation, and a safe space to express and process their emotions. If their emotional strength is strong, we can encourage emotional expression and provide opportunities for emotional growth and self-reflection.

13. *Degree of vulnerability*: Understanding whether the individual is more vulnerable or grounded guides our approach to creating a supportive environment. If they are more vulnerable, we can provide additional emotional support, reassurance, and a predictable routine. If they are more grounded, we can encourage autonomy, problem-solving skills, and independence while still being available for guidance.

14. *Communication of needs and feelings*: Being aware of whether the individual is unable or able to effectively communicate their needs and feelings helps us ensure their voices are heard. If they are unable, we can employ alternative communication methods and create a

supportive environment that encourages expression. If they are able, we can promote open communication, active listening, and validate their experiences.

15. *Community inclusion:* Observing whether the individual feels excluded or included in the community informs our efforts to foster a sense of belonging and social integration. If they feel excluded, we can facilitate community connections, promote participation in group activities, and create opportunities for social interactions. If they feel included, we can strengthen their sense of belonging and encourage them to engage actively within the community.

16. *Degree of support needed:* Understanding whether the individual requires significant or ordinary support guides our role as a skilled companion. If they require significant support, we can provide additional assistance, adaptations, and individualized interventions. If they require ordinary support, we can encourage independence while being available for guidance and support when needed.

These 16 areas of reciprocation can be used as a reference for observing, identifying, and interpreting how the individual is communicating, responding, and engaging as they use their own tools of presence, eyes, words, and hands. Adjustments to the multi-sensory environment require flexibility by the skilled companion, when the need arises for re-creating interactions that adapt to the needs and preferences of the individual.

Interactions in the MSE room focus on an individual's unique needs, supporting experiential learning for social-emotional awareness and growth, contributing to the individual's overall well-being and quality of life.

A CULTURE OF HOPE

Experiencing the quality of *trust* in human connections (companionship and a sense of community) plants the seed for a culture of hope. Trust is the initial step and first stage that takes root in the social-emotional foundation that essentially supports all experiential learning and the processing (determining the value) of meaningful moments.

In the MSE room, a culture of hope is created from the social formation of how we are able to build relationships that engage others in discovering their value and participating with their skilled companion in the creating of meaningful moments. Through experiential learning, elements of both the relationship-building and of the MSE room sustain support for the whole process of social-emotional development.

While we acknowledge the importance of and understand the purpose for addressing old memories and experiences, the focus for the skilled companion is to provide a nurturing and supportive environment that vitalizes the creation of new, moral memories. By doing so, the skilled companion assists the individual in rewriting their narrative, emphasizing their strengths, and creating a culture of hope and possibility. With new moral memories being sown, creating meaningful moments looks at present and future possibilities, no longer limited by the brokenness and isolation of unresolved past experiences.

Through the creating and integrating of new moral memories, the individual can become empowered in the re-forming of their narrative, and become aware the transformative nature of their existence, enriching their overall well-being and quality-of-life.

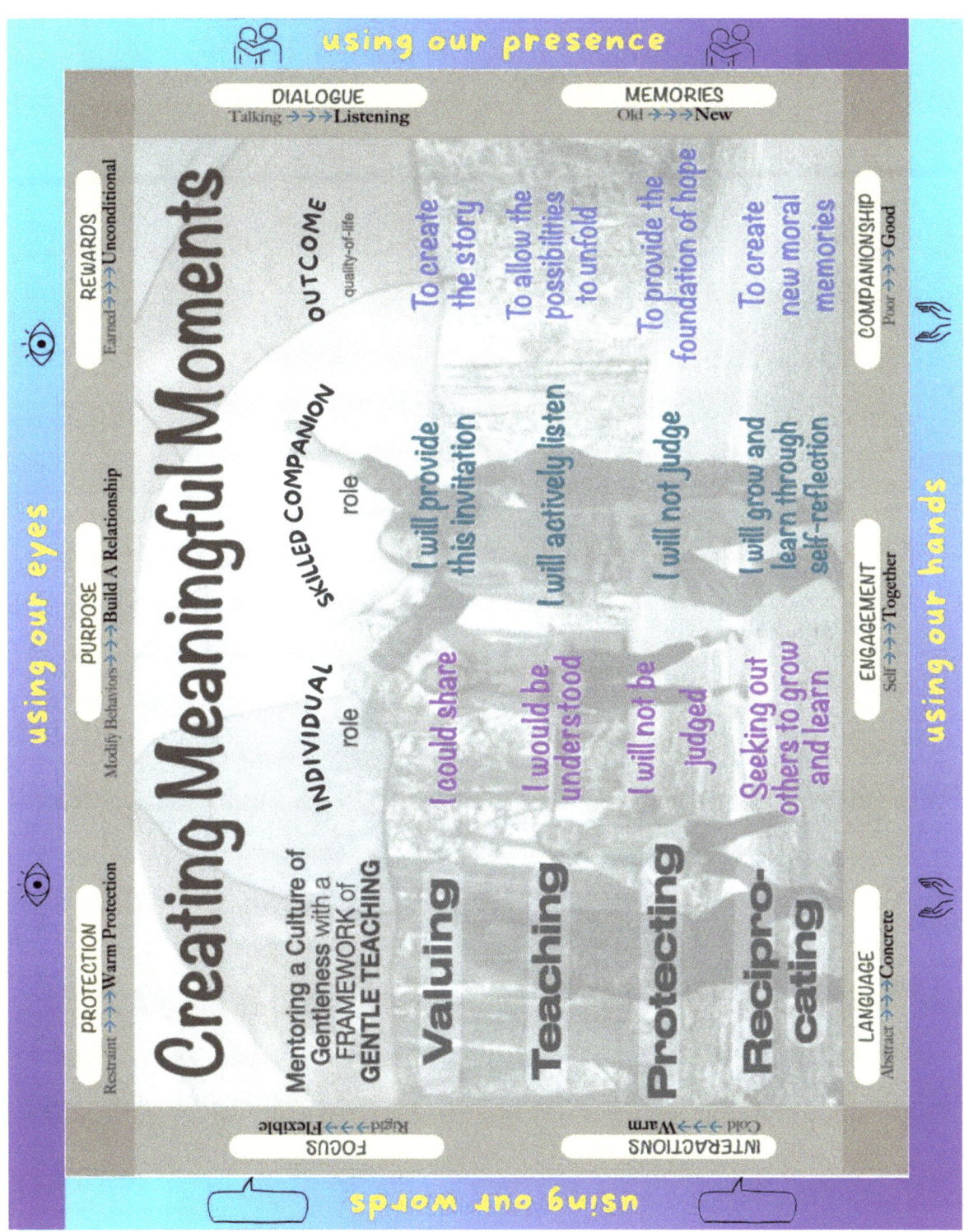

HUMAN CONNECTION

The trusted relationship lays the foundation for a culture of hope and the blossoming of companionship. With companionship, the human connection within the interactions unfolds the invitation for creating meaningful moments. Active listening, use of Our Tools for communication and dialogue, understanding, compassion, and encouragement all facilitate the overall experience and quality-of-life outcomes for the individual.

Accessibility to interactions and the relationally dynamic elements that the MSE room provides is essential for growth in social-emotional awareness, self-regulation, and development. Human beings learn how to be human from other human beings.

The relational dynamic (*dyad*) is critical for the valuing of the individual and for creating meaning; concepts that relate and connect with the individual. While this dynamic can naturally occur in families and other social structures, its accessibility is often out of reach for marginalized and/or traumatized individuals. In the role of a skilled companion (or anyone working in the field of social services), it is essential that the social-emotional aspect of human awareness and growth is acknowledged, validated, and integrated.

It is the human connection that elevates the MSE experience and makes it genuine and meaningful. The human connection is the heart of MSE interactions. The relationship-building framework of Gentle Teaching in the MSE room gives structure and movement to the experiential processes within the multi-sensory environment.

The MSE room provides a safe and stimulating environment where individuals can explore and engage their senses. It allows them to relax, experience pleasure, and connect with their inner selves. But the meaningful connections happen when we, as skilled companions, can connect with empathy and compassion.

By taking the time to understand each person's unique needs, preferences, and abilities, the skilled companion can tailor the MSE experience to create an authentic, personalized journey for the individual. It is in these moments of connection that we foster trust, build rapport, and create a space where individuals feel understood and valued.

The role of the skilled companion extends beyond simply providing a physical environment and implementing MSE techniques. Our presence is to create meaningful connections that touch the lives of those we serve. Our ability to empathize, listen, and respond to emotional and sensory cues, allows us to co-create an experience that goes beyond the surface.

In the MSE room, we have the privilege of witnessing the profound impact our mentoring presence can have on an individual's well-being. It is a reminder of the transformative power of human connection and the quality-of-life difference we can make in the lives of others. With the compassionate and trusted relationship of the skilled companion, creating meaningful moments cultivates an environment where individuals can inclusively and authentically thrive on their path of being and becoming human.

SEE worksheet for SECTION 8

25. *GIFTS: ~ Reciprocation ~*
          ~ Culture of Hope ~
          ~ Human Connection ~

Notes:

Notes:

ABOUT THE AUTHOR

Dr. Anthony (Tony) M. McCrovitz, Ph.D., is the Executive Director of the Quality of Life Institute, Inc., a nonprofit committed to enhancing the well-being of individuals facing various challenges. As a Licensed Psychologist and Mental Health  Counselor, he specializes in child development and holistic, bio-psychosocial approaches.

Throughout his career, Dr. McCrovitz has been a dedicated advocate for individuals with disabilities, focusing on breaking down cultural and community barriers. He's known for developing a Quality-of-Life Model™ that integrates the relationship-building principles of Gentle Teaching into his work. His commitment to the sharing of knowledge and resource materials for direct service providers has led him to collaborate globally, working with organizations and professionals to improve inclusive learning communities that support both personal and professional growth.

In addition to his leadership at Quality of Life Institute, Dr. McCrovitz has taught developmental psychology and lifespan courses at various colleges and universities. He holds a Ph.D. in I/O Psychology from Walden University, a respecialization in Clinical Psychology from Adler Professional School of Psychology, an MBA from Indiana Wesleyan University, and a master's degree in pastoral counseling from Loyola University of Chicago. Other books he has authored include "Anthony's Backpack: A Child's Journey into Gentleness" (2010) and "Return to Gentleness: Journeying with Gentle Teaching" (2021).

Dr. McCrovitz is an active board member of the Gentle Teaching International community, the International Snoezelen-MSE Association (ISNA-MSE.org), and the Institute of Multi-Sensory Environments (I-MSE.org), presenting internationally on topics connecting neuroscience and sensory integration to facilitate inclusive learning for all, creating sustainable outcomes with quality of life solutions.

www.ingramcontent.com/pod-product-compliance
Lightning Source LLC
Chambersburg PA
CBHW061928290426
44113CB00024B/2839